Understanding the 2000 Election

Abner Greene

Understanding the 2000 Election

A Guide to the Legal Battles That Decided
the Presidency

New York University Press • New York and London

To the memory of my father, Phil Greene

NEW YORK UNIVERSITY PRESS
New York and London

Library of Congress Cataloging-in-Publication Data
Greene, Abner, 1960–
Understanding the 2000 election : a guide to the legal battles that
decided the presidency / Abner Greene.
p.   cm.
Includes index.
ISBN 0-8147-3148-1 (cloth : alk. paper)
1. Bush, George W. (George Walker), 1946– —Trials, litigation, etc.
2. Gore, Albert, 1948– —Trials, litigation, etc. 3. Contested elections—
United States. 4. Contested elections—Florida. 5. Presidents—
United States—Election—2000.   I. Title.
KF5074.2 .G74 2001
324.973'0929—dc21   2001002835

New York University Press books are printed on acid-free paper,
and their binding materials are chosen for strength and durability.

Manufactured in the United States of America
10 9 8 7 6 5 4 3 2 1

Contents

Introduction

Only once has the United States Supreme Court ended a presidential election. Only once has a presidential election come down to several hundred votes, in one state. Only once has a candidate won the presidency while losing the popular vote by more than 500,000 votes. The 2000 presidential election featured all of this, and more. It was instant history, and it will be studied by historians, lawyers, political scientists, biographers, media critics, and others for years to come.

This book offers an understandable, comprehensive guide to the legal battles that finally gave Governor George W. Bush the presidency five weeks after election night. Many legal issues captured the nation's attention during those five late autumn weeks. For most of the time, the focus was on Vice President Al Gore's insistence on manual recounts of punch-card ballots. Two cases involving manual recounts went through the Florida Supreme Court and up to the United States Supreme Court. Even amid the storm over manual counting, other issues demanded attention as well. In particular, courts resolved the Palm Beach County "butterfly ballot" case, challenging the legality of the ballot format, and two potentially devastating cases involving Republican Party alteration of absentee ballot request forms. In the background, lurking, was the Florida legislature, seemingly prepared to deliver Florida's electoral votes to Governor Jeb Bush's older brother. And off in the distance was the U.S. Congress, ready to play an uncertain role if the electoral matter remained unresolved into January 2001. This book covers all of these issues in detail not available in the newspapers or on television. At the same time, it breaks down their legal complexity, so lawyers and nonlawyers alike can follow along.

Everyone knew it would be a close election. All the national polls showed either Bush or Gore ahead by a smidgen going into election day. All the scenarios for electoral vote counting showed a similarly close race, with some pundits predicting that Bush might win the popular vote but lose the electoral vote and the presidency to Gore. (One of the many wonderful ironies of the election was that the pundits were 180 degrees wrong—Gore won the popular vote but lost the electoral vote and the presidency to Bush.) For Gore to win, he needed almost all the close states. Early on election night, it appeared he was winning them. Michigan fell his way, then Pennsylvania. And when the networks began calling Florida for Gore, it looked as if the White House was his.

But a funny thing happened on the way to a Gore White House—the networks had erred in calling Florida. Some Gore supporters say that the networks did not err, that the exit polls showing Gore to be the victor in the Sunshine State were accurate, and that only bizarre irregularities such as the confusing Palm Beach County butterfly ballot resulted in a Bush victory. Whatever the case, the networks yanked Florida from the Gore column as midnight neared on election night and put it back into the undecided column. One A.M. passed, then 2 A.M., and the race was still too close to call. Gore picked up the key states of Wisconsin, Washington, and Iowa; Bush countered by prevailing in Arkansas and in Gore's home state of Tennessee. Florida's twenty-five electoral votes, it appeared, would be critical for either candidate. If either could pick up Florida, he would be the next president.

Then, after 2 A.M., the networks called Florida, and the White House, for Bush. They pronounced him the forty-third president. Gore phoned Bush to tell him he would concede, and the celebration for the Texas governor was about to begin in Austin. But on the way to give his concession speech at War Memorial Plaza in downtown Nashville, Gore learned that Florida was much closer than the networks thought, close enough for him to demand a mandatory statewide recount. According to well-publicized reports, the following conversation occurred: Gore phoned Bush and retracted his concession. Bush was quite agitated by this, and Gore responded, "You don't have to be snippy about it." When Bush said that his brother, Governor Jeb Bush of Florida, had assured him that Florida was a GOP win, Gore countered, "Your younger brother is not the ultimate authority on this." America woke up the day after the election with the presidency hanging in the balance and with teams of Democratic and Republican lawyers flying into Florida to begin managing the recount process.

Over the ensuing five weeks, that counting continued, only to end with the instant landmark Supreme Court decision, *Bush v. Gore.* Bush had won Florida by 537 votes, and the presidency by 271 electoral votes to Gore's 267.[1] This book examines every major legal battle involved in resolving the election, plus other legal issues related to the election of a U.S. president. Chapter 1 discusses the process of electing the president through the electoral vote. On election night, what mattered legally? What would give either Bush or Gore the White House? Here I explain the difference between the electoral and the popular vote. The electoral vote is an oddity, and I explore its role in the text of the U.S.

Constitution, as well as provide some historical background. That history includes the founding design of the Constitution and recounts the few times prior to 2000 that the winner of the popular vote did not prevail in the electoral vote. I also lay out some of the current debate over whether we should keep the electoral college. By the end of election night, the 2000 presidency was in doubt not because of the popular vote—Al Gore had definitely prevailed—but because of the electoral vote. Neither candidate had clearly gained the 270 electoral votes needed.

The centerpiece of the legal battles was Gore's attempt to recount thousands of ballots by hand. Part I of the book examines the legal issues surrounding the hand counts. Chapter 2 provides the background for what is to follow. The GOP waged a persistent campaign to discredit manual recounts. But Florida law, and the law in many other states, clearly provides for counting by hand. For example, as became known early on, Bush had signed into Texas law a provision for manual recounts. Caselaw from many states backs up what appears in the statutes: In close elections, human beings are entrusted to inspect ballots, and votes are counted on the basis of various indicia of a voter's intent. But the law in most states, Florida included, does not provide clear rules on what ballot markings count as evidence of a voter's intent. This lack of guidance ultimately became the key to the election, and to Gore's demise. This chapter discusses the purpose of hand counts, surveys their use in Florida and elsewhere, examines the various types of chads—those little pieces of the punchcard that do or don't fall out when you punch them—and looks at how to figure out a voter's intent depending on how the ballot-card is punched.

Florida law clearly says that counties must submit vote totals by one week after the election, and Secretary of State Katherine Harris insisted that November 14 was indeed the end of vote counting. Gore's challenge to that position led to the first major battle in the Florida Supreme Court. After a trial judge ruled that Harris had not abused her discretion in refusing to accept any manual recounts submitted after November 14, the Florida Supreme Court unanimously reversed and gave a major victory to Gore. Chapter 3 explains the conflicts within the Florida election code, shows how the Florida high court resolved those conflicts, and describes the battle that remained.

The hand counting continued until November 26, the deadline set by the Florida high court. With Secretary of State Harris certifying the election for Bush (who held a 537-vote lead at the time), the stage was set for Gore to challenge that certification. He did so by filing a "contest" action, and by using a devastatingly simple and potentially powerful argument. Florida law allows a losing candidate to contest an election by showing a "rejection of a number of legal votes sufficient to change or place in doubt the result of the election." That statutory language—enacted in 1999—had never been interpreted by a Florida court. Gore argued that both human beings and machines had rejected votes. Gore wanted some votes added to his column, and he wanted other ballots counted by hand. Bush responded that Gore's reading of the statute made no sense; he argued that a losing candidate has to show that officials acted illegally or, at the very least, abused their discretion. The Florida Supreme Court, in its second, even more dramatic, ruling, held for Gore by a 4-3 vote. Chapter 4 explores the powerful arguments on both sides and explains how the stage was set for the U.S. Supreme Court.

In many ways, the ultimate U.S. Supreme Court ruling was anticipated by a small group of judges in a separate lawsuit that made its way to the federal court of appeals in Atlanta, the Eleventh Circuit. Chapter 5 considers the lawsuit that Bush and some Florida citizens filed days after the election, takes the reader through the dismissal of that case by Federal Judge Middlebrooks, and finishes with the Eleventh Circuit's affirmance of

Middlebrooks's decision. Despite that affirmance, four conservative judges wrote strongly against the constitutionality of the manual recounts, and their opinions echoed in the final U.S. Supreme Court opinions.

Part I ends on the precipice of the final U.S. Supreme Court intervention. But that case was not just about the constitutional status of manual counting. It also contained another thread, which is the subject of Part II: the Bush accusation that the Florida Supreme Court had usurped the prerogatives of the Florida Legislature and thereby violated federal law and the federal Constitution. This was always a fairly astonishing argument, for it is well settled that federal courts generally defer to interpretation of state law by state courts. But in the setting of a presidential election, a different kind of supervision of state courts is required, or so Bush argued.

At the heart of the Bush challenge to the Florida Supreme Court's interpretation of state law was the argument that the Florida high court had legislated instead of interpreted, had in essence rewritten state law. There were two parts to this argument. The first relied on an obscure section of federal law—section 5 of the third volume of the United States Code. That section ensures that if a state resolves any judicial challenge (or "contest") regarding electors by six days before those electors must cast their votes for president, and if it does so through law in existence on the date of the election, then the electors determined through that judicial contest may not be challenged afterward. In other words, section 5 creates a "safe harbor" for those electors. I cover in chapter 9 the aspect of the safe-harbor provision that deals with completing a judicial contest in a timely fashion; that part of the law turned out to be critical to the ultimate Bush victory. In chapter 6, I examine the aspect of the safe-harbor provision that focuses on resolving judicial contests under law in existence on election day, and Bush's claim that the

Florida Supreme Court violated this principle by rewriting Florida law, rather than just interpreting it. The second part of Bush's argument that the Florida high court had legislated rather than interpreted pointed to the U.S. Constitution. In this chapter, I discuss Bush's contention that the Florida Supreme Court had unconstitutionally stripped the Florida legislature of its Article II, Section 1 power under the U.S. Constitution to determine the manner of choosing that state's electors.

Connected to this concern was the argument that in the setting of presidential elections, a state court may not rely on a state constitution if doing so would override a choice made by the state legislature. This is an inversion of the normal order of things, in which constitutions trump statutes in cases of conflict. But U.S. Supreme Court Justice Antonin Scalia, during the first U.S. Supreme Court oral argument, pressed hard on this issue. I explore it in chapter 7.

The first time the U.S. Supreme Court reviewed the Florida Supreme Court, the constitutionality of hand counts was not at issue. But the other Bush attacks on the Florida high court were. Rather than resolve them, the U.S. high court sent the matter back to the Florida Supreme Court for clarification. I cover this in chapter 8. Specifically, the U.S. Supreme Court asked the Florida Supreme Court to clarify whether and to what extent it had relied on its own constitution and also asked it whether and to what extent it had thought about the safe-harbor section of federal law. The Florida Supreme Court responded to this request for clarification one night before the U.S. Supreme Court ended the election. And, although the Florida high court response attracted little attention, some of its language proved central to the ultimate Bush victory.

After the Florida Supreme Court ruled for Gore in his challenge to Bush's certification as the Florida winner, manual counting resumed the next day across Florida. Quickly, though, the

U.S. Supreme Court pounced and, in a momentous midafternoon 5-4 ruling, stopped the counting by issuing a "stay" order. After oral arguments two days later, the nation's high court took only one more day to end the election. By the same 5-4 vote, the Court ruled that the hand counting could not resume. Chapter 9 (which makes up Part III of the book) explores the six opinions issued—the unsigned opinion for the Court, the concurrence by Chief Justice William Rehnquist, and the dissents by Justices John Paul Stevens, David Souter, Ruth Bader Ginsburg, and Stephen Breyer. Only three Justices bought the full range of Bush's arguments—only Rehnquist, Scalia, and Clarence Thomas agreed with Bush that the Florida Supreme Court had usurped the prerogatives of the Florida legislature. But seven Justices—those three plus the other two so-called conservatives, Justices Sandra Day O'Connor and Anthony Kennedy, as well as two of the so-called liberals, Souter and Breyer—agreed that the Florida scheme for counting ballots by hand was constitutionally deficient. In particular, they pointed to the vague "voter's intent" standard for reading ballots and to the failure of Florida law to insist that all counties use the same rules to determine what counts as evidence of voter intent. These flaws—a vague standard plus the absence of common criteria for fleshing out that standard—pose too great a risk of bias, conscious or not, the Court reasoned, and pose too great a risk that voters in different counties will have their votes counted differently.

But what should the Court do with such a holding? Here the center of the Court shattered, with Souter and Breyer insisting that the matter be sent back to Florida for the opportunity to settle on clear, common standards for vote counting, so long as the counting could be concluded by December 18, when the electors across the country must cast their votes. That would have given Florida six days. O'Connor and Kennedy, however, disagreed and, joined by Rehnquist, Scalia, and Thomas, held that the election must end immediately, that night, December 12. The reason for this dramatic order—which handed the presidency to Bush—was a questionable reading of the Florida Supreme Court's discussion of the safe-harbor provision. According to the U.S. Supreme Court majority, the Florida Supreme Court had itself said that the Florida legislature wanted to ensure the safe harbor for the Florida electors, wanted to make sure the judicial contest was concluded no later than December 12, so that there could be no challenge to Florida's electoral slate. I explore both what the U.S. Supreme Court said and what the Florida Supreme Court actually said regarding that crucial December 12 date.

Although the U.S. Supreme Court ended the election on December 12, there were other legal issues brewing during the five-week postelection period, and the remainder of the book discusses them. I begin, in Part IV, with two lawsuits that lurked on the periphery but that had the potential to damage Bush's run at the White House. First, in chapter 10, I discuss the bizarre situation in Palm Beach County. It is indisputable that the unusual physical design of the ballot in Palm Beach County led many voters either to vote for the wrong candidate or to vote for two candidates instead of one, voiding the ballot. But was the "butterfly ballot" illegal under Florida law, or just confusing? And if it was illegal, what remedy could a court order? Could a court order a new election, a "revote," in the words of the many protestors? A trial judge ruled No on the revote question; the Florida Supreme Court, in a brief, cryptic opinion, threw out the trial judge's opinion but resolved the matter similarly against the Democratic plaintiffs, holding that the butterfly ballot was in substantial compliance with Florida election law.

Chapter 11 deals with two lawsuits that many commentators thought posed the greatest danger to Bush. In two counties, GOP personnel were permitted to alter absentee ballot applications after they had been rejected by county elections officials as incomplete. In both counties, the GOP operatives added voter registration numbers that the GOP printers had inadvertently left off the preprinted forms. In both counties, no other incomplete absentee ballot applications were rescued. Florida law does not authorize political party personnel to complete absentee ballot applications. That was not in dispute. The questions were whether such behavior constituted "substantial noncompliance with statutory voting procedures," the standard laid down by Florida's high court for contesting an election, and, if so, whether it was appropriate to invalidate all of the counties' absentee ballot votes, as plaintiffs requested. In both cases, the judges ruled that the violations were not serious enough to warrant a remedy. The Florida Supreme Court affirmed both rulings.

Finally, in Part V, I discuss the roles of the Florida legislature and the U.S. Congress. Chapter 12 lays out the arguments for and against the intervention of the Florida legislature in this election. The Republicans argued that the Constitution and a federal statute permitted, and perhaps required, legislative intervention, at least if the election remained unresolved after the safe-harbor date of December 12. The Democrats argued that once the Florida legislature had, by law, delegated to the citizens of Florida the power to choose the state's presidential electors, the legislature had no appropriate role in the selection.

Although the U.S. Congress wasn't ultimately involved in picking the president, federal law and the U.S. Constitution envision circumstances in which the Congress would play a role. In particular, federal law gives Congress the power to choose between competing slates of electors, and the Constitution gives the House and the Senate the power to select the president and the vice president, respectively, if no candidate gains an electoral college majority. I discuss the scenarios that didn't come to pass, but well could have, in chapter 13.

In the Afterword, I defend the legal process against attack

from critics who contend that it is nothing but politics. Some hold this view about law generally; others made more pointed arguments about the role of law in resolving the 2000 presidential election. Against both challenges, I offer a defense for law as a domain of reason. Just as politics provides a buffer zone between citizens, defusing potential violence, so does law streamline the rough and tumble of politics into a forum of principle, which exists even amid the most contentious political strife.

Background

1. Winning the Presidency

The Electoral Vote

The election could have ended quickly. As election night wore on, it became clear that more people across the country had voted for Al Gore than for George W. Bush. Gore, that is, had won the "popular vote." He was more popular, but that wasn't enough to make him president. We don't elect the president as we elect virtually all other officeholders. Instead, we have something called the "electoral vote." To win the presidency, a candidate needs a majority of these votes. By the morning after the 2000 election, neither candidate had the 270 electoral votes needed to constitute such a majority. Florida, with its twenty-five electoral votes, would give the presidency to one of these men, but, although Bush was ahead in Florida, his lead was too small for the state to declare him the winner. This chapter explains the basic rules regarding the electoral vote, explores why we have such an unusual system for picking the president, and considers whether the electoral method is likely to change any time soon.

The Constitution of the United States creates a system of electors to pick the president. When we vote for president, we are technically voting for other people—die-hard party loyalists, often state or local officials—who are committed to voting for the candidate we want. So when we vote for "Al Gore" or "George W. Bush," we are voting for Gore or Bush electors who have been lined up to cast their electoral votes for those candidates. Some states require electors to vote for the candidate to whom they have stated allegiance; other states do not. But, even in the states that require electors to be faithful, those requirements are enforced only after the fact, so even in those states an elector can be unfaithful and face the consequences afterward. There have been few instances of faithless electors, and none that has changed the outcome of an election.

Each state receives as many electoral votes as it has members of Congress. So each state starts off with two electoral votes, representing the two senators from each state, and then adds as many electoral votes as it has members of the House of Representatives. The Constitution gives states with smaller populations disproportionate clout in the Senate, and this carries over to the electoral votes from small states. If representation in both Houses of Congress were strictly according to population, California (the state with the most people) and Wyoming (the state with the fewest people) would not both have two senators, and those states would not each start with a core of two electoral votes. Although it might seem that California, with fifty-five electoral votes (reflecting the updated 2000 census data), has vastly more electoral clout than Wyoming, with three, if electoral votes were apportioned according to population, the ratio would be about 205:3 rather than 55:3.[1]

Although Congress sets the date for presidential elections,[2] the Constitution grants state legislatures the power to determine the "manner" of selecting electors.[3] Today, in each state, citizens choose electors by popular vote, but state legislatures could insist that electors be chosen another way. For example, a state legislature could, by law, delegate to itself the power to pick the presidential electors. And, for many years, many states did just that.

State legislatures also may tinker with the way electors are apportioned. So, although forty-eight states currently give all their electors to the presidential candidate who receives the most votes on election day, two states (Maine and Nebraska) use a different method, each awarding two electors to the statewide winner and the remaining electors to the winner in each congressional district. A state could choose to award all of its electors by congressional district, or it could choose to award its electors in proportion to the popular vote in the state. The big point is that state legislatures have broad power to determine the "manner" of selecting electors.

To win the presidency, a candidate needs a majority of the electoral votes from across the country.[4] Currently there are 538 electoral votes in total—100 representing the number of seats in the Senate; 435 representing the number of seats in the House; and three extra electoral votes for the District of Columbia, which, although it has no representation in Congress, was given three electoral votes via the Twenty-Third Amendment to the Constitution, which was ratified in 1961. So a candidate needs 270 electoral votes to attain the majority needed to be elected president. If there is a tie (269-269), or if for some other reason a candidate fails to win a majority (for example, if a third-party candidate wins some electoral votes), then the presidency is decided under special rules set forth in the Twelfth Amendment to the Constitution. Under this amendment, the House of Representatives picks the president from the top three electoral vote-getters. Each state's House delegation gets one vote.[5] If a state has more Democratic than Republican members in the House, it will vote for the Democratic presidential candidate; if its House delegation is majority Republican, it will vote for the Republican candidate. If a state's House delegation is evenly divided and no one breaks party ranks, then that state will not cast a vote. To win, a candidate must receive votes from a majority of state delegations (twenty-six, currently). If no candidate for vice president has won an electoral vote majority, the Senate, voting by individual member, picks the vice president from the two highest electoral vote-getters. A majority vote (fifty-one, currently) is needed to prevail. Thus, it is possible for the House to select a president from one party, while the Senate selects a vice president from another party. The District of Columbia, although it has three electoral votes, plays no role if the election is thrown into the House and the Senate.

So that's the system, and it does seem mighty strange. Why do we have it? To answer that question, one must look back to the framing of the Constitution. When the framers met in Philadelphia in the summer of 1787 to draft the Constitution, one of the issues that plagued them throughout was establishing a method for picking a president. In fact, when the conflict over this issue finally ended, James Wilson, of Pennsylvania, remarked that it had been "the most difficult issue of all on which we have to decide."[6] For most of the summer, the framers debated whether to give Congress the power to pick the president or whether to give the people, through popular vote, that power. In vote after vote on this issue, the supporters of congressional selection prevailed.[7] They were concerned that the people would not be able to discern the best person for the job. Members of Congress, they thought, would have better insight into the qualities needed to be the chief executive.[8] But those who believed that citizens should choose their president fought back. They argued that confidence in the president would be greater if the people could select their own leader. They also were concerned that the president would be subservient to Congress if he were dependent on its support for his appointment and possible reappointment.[9] As with many other issues discussed during the Constitutional Convention, the framers thought about matters as a package.[10] With respect to the presidency, four issues were intertwined: the powers of the office, the length of a presidential term, whether a president could stand for reelection, and how the president would be selected. For much of the summer, the package on the table combined congressional appointment with no term limitation, and, for the supporters of election by the citizenry, this was too much to bear. By allowing a president to stand for reelection and giving Congress the power to choose the president, the Constitution threatened to make Congress vastly more powerful than the president, or so these framers argued. The president would be constantly trying to please Congress, to win another term.

All along, as a possible compromise, there was the electoral college idea.[11] (Note that the phrase "electoral college" doesn't actually appear in the Constitution!) Although it is sometimes said that the framers chose the electoral college because they thought the electors would be wise people who would deliberate and filter out partisan preference, in fact that was not a principal defense. Rather, the electoral college concept lacked the vices of the other two models[12]—Congress would no longer be all-powerful over the president, and the masses would not be in position to mess things up by picking someone who wasn't fit for the job. Thus, late in the summer, after a majority had voted many times to vest selection of the president in Congress, a special committee sent to iron out various constitutional issues reported back, and it had adopted the idea of using electors.[13] The full convention accepted the proposal,[14] relieved to be rid of the seemingly endless debate over how a president should be selected. The one thorny issue that remained was what to do in case no candidate received a majority of electoral votes, as many framers expected would happen often. The initial proposal was to let the Senate decide, but that was thought to give too much power to the small states, which have disproportionate influence in the Senate.

Moreover, many framers objected that, because the Senate had so few members, power over presidential selection would be dangerously concentrated in the hands of a small group. The alternative—letting the House decide, with each member getting one vote—was rejected by the framers from the small states. Finally, a compromise was reached: The House would decide, but with each state's House delegation getting one vote.[15] This way the small states got something (each state was represented equally in the voting), but, by placing the choice in the significantly larger House of Representatives, the framers avoided concentrating power in the hands of the smaller senatorial group.

Although the records of the Constitutional Convention reveal that the electoral college idea was a compromise based in political necessity, Alexander Hamilton in the *Federalist Papers* managed to present a case for the electoral vote based in principle.[16] He advanced three main arguments. First, there would be no pre-established body of electors. Instead, electors would be appointed for the limited task of electing a president in a given year. That made corruption and other improper influence less likely. Second, because the electors would be few in number and would be people of discernment, they would be well situated to analyze whether the candidates were of presidential timber. Third, because voters would choose a number of electors and would do so state by state, political energies would be decentralized and thus less likely to explode. Like other arguments in the *Federalist Papers,* Hamilton's argument for the electoral college was a smashing piece of political rhetoric aimed at ensuring ratification of the Constitution.

Thus, we have a system for choosing a president that is the result of two constitutional compromises, plus some clever salesmanship. On principle, the electoral college was no one's first choice.

And, although the framers thought that elections might often end up in Congress, with no candidate having received a majority of the electoral votes, presidential elections have gone to Congress under the constitutional mechanism only twice. One of those instances was the result of a problem with the electoral system as originally adopted. Under the original Constitution, the system required each elector to vote for two candidates. The candidate with the highest number of votes would become president, while the candidate with the second highest number of votes would become vice president. The problem was that if two candidates ran as a team, one ostensibly for president and the other for vice president, electors might cast their votes equally for both members of that team, and then neither candidate would have a higher vote total. That is what happened in 1800, when Thomas Jefferson and Aaron Burr both received the same number of electoral votes. The election went to the House, which selected Jefferson for president and Burr for vice president. The Twelfth Amendment, ratified in 1804, corrected the glitch in the original Constitution by directing electors to make "distinct lists" of votes for president and votes for vice president.

The other election thrown into the House took place in 1820, when five candidates received electoral votes, but none achieved a majority. After some horse trading, John Quincy Adams (the only president's son before George W. Bush to reach the presidency) prevailed. The 1820 election also represented the first of four times that the popular vote winner lost the electoral vote. In 1820, after election day returns were in, Andrew Jackson had received the most popular votes and the most electoral votes, but he lacked an electoral majority and lost to Adams in the House. (He got his revenge by defeating Adams four years later and went on to win a second term, as well.)

The 1876 election was the second in which popular vote winner lost the electoral vote. That was the now famous Hayes-Tilden election. Samuel Tilden, the Democratic governor of New York, was ahead in the popular vote after election day and needed only one more electoral vote to beat Rutherford B. Hayes, the Republican governor of Ohio, for the presidency. Tilden would have prevailed if any one of three states—Florida, Louisiana, or South Carolina—had gone his way. But all three states—southern states, during Reconstruction—sent two slates of electors to Washington.[17] In Florida, the courts certified the Tilden slate, while the governor certified the Hayes slate. Louisiana had two sitting governments, one Democratic and one Republican. South Carolina certified only a Republican slate, but a Democratic one presented itself, as well. After much wheeling and dealing, a congressionally appointed electoral commission awarded all the electoral votes from the three states to Hayes. In exchange, not only did Hayes give plum executive positions to Democrats, but he also agreed to take other actions that effectively ended Reconstruction.[18]

Other than John Quincy Adams and Hayes—and, now, George W. Bush—the only president to win election despite losing the popular vote was Benjamin Harrison. In 1888, he wrested the presidency away from Grover Cleveland. Cleveland came back four years later and recaptured the White House, becoming the only president to win two terms nonconsecutively.

So should the electoral college be scrapped? The arguments in favor of ending it, and electing presidents via popular vote, are strong. The leading argument is that our president should be the person whom most citizens support. That might not be a majority, of course, because strong third-party candidates can ensure that the popular-vote winner falls short of that mark. But it would still accord with how virtually every other officeholder is elected. It would also accord with important shifts in voting rights since the framing of the Constitution. In the late 1700s, the vote was held almost entirely by white males, property ownership often played a role in voting eligibility, and state legislatures chose senators for the U.S. Congress. The electoral college idea fit better then—the idea of blocking a direct vote by the people accorded with a conception of "citizen" that didn't envision blacks or women voting and that didn't comprehend the concept of "one person, one vote." The Fifteenth Amendment, ratified in 1870, ensured that the right to vote could not be denied on the basis of race. In 1913, the Seventeenth Amendment switched senatorial elections from state legislatures to the citizenry. Women gained a constitutional right to vote via the Nineteenth Amendment, ratified in 1920. Poll taxes—qualifications based on wealth—were constitutionally banned by the Twenty-Fourth Amendment, ratified in 1964. And the voting age was lowered to eighteen through the Twenty-Sixth Amendment, ratified in 1971. The electoral college just doesn't fit any more within our expanded landscape of voting rights.

The electoral college also exacerbates the inequality present in the structure of the U.S. Senate. It is true that the Constitution would not have been ratified without the compromise establishing a House of Representatives whose membership is apportioned according to population and a Senate that has two members per state, regardless of population. And it is also true that the only item in the Constitution that may not be amended without consent of all affected is the equal number of senators per state. Yes, that's right. At the end of Article V of the Constitution, which sets forth procedures for amending the Constitution, we see the following: "no State, without its consent, shall be deprived of its equal suffrage in the Senate."[19] But the electoral vote is not similarly locked in. It replicates the inequality of the two-Senators-per-state rule and thereby exaggerates the impact of smaller states in presidential voting.

Some argue, however, that this effect is healthy, that presidential candidates should not ignore states with smaller populations, and that the president is the leader of the entire nation, small-population states as well as large-population states. If we move to a popular vote, these advocates contend, presidential candidates would spend time only in states with large populations. One response to these arguments is to look at a list of states visited by Gore and Bush. The visits were overwhelmingly to states with larger populations, because even with the "Senate effect" in the electoral vote, the large-population states still yield the greatest electoral prizes. In elections thought to be close, candidates need every vote, and if they can pick up votes in the small-population states they will certainly try to do so. And the argument that the president represents the entire nation, although true, must not be seen as an argument for representing land instead of people. That concept was discarded with the important U.S. Supreme Court decisions of the early 1960s that insisted on "one person, one vote"[20]—that representation must be in accord with population, not land. The U.S. Senate is, of course, the constitutionally locked-in exception to this principle.

Some argue against shifting to the popular vote by pointing to what happened in 2000 in Florida. Granted, that was a mess, these electoral-vote supporters contend, but at least it was a mess focused on one state. If we move to the popular vote, and an election is very tight, then we might see recounts requested around the country, and that would be a nightmare. Indeed, in an extremely close election that might happen, but there are various responses. First, the election would have to be closer than any election in memory. Gore's margin in the popular vote exceeded 500,000; in the closest twentieth-century election, John F. Kennedy beat Richard Nixon in 1960 by just over 100,000 votes. It would take an awful lot of shifted votes in a recount to disrupt even those popular vote margins, and therefore it is unlikely that recounts would be sought nationwide. Second, a candidate would still have to satisfy the various state standards for requesting recounts. Third, if we move toward a national system of presidential voting, as many are urging, the error rate from vote tabulation might decrease dramatically, eliminating the need for recounts. Finally, even if on a rare occasion recounts in many states might be required, perhaps that should be seen as the cost of a more democratically principled system of choosing a president.

Despite the strength of the arguments for eliminating the electoral college, it isn't going to happen any time soon, and it probably will never happen. To propose an amendment to the Constitution, two-thirds of the members of each House of Congress have to agree, or two-thirds of the state legislatures have to call a convention for proposing amendments. If an amendment is proposed, either by Congress or through a convention, then three-quarters of the states must vote to ratify the amendment, either through vote of the state legislatures or by state conventions, with Congress choosing the mode of ratification. That means that thirty-eight states (37½, actually, rounded up to thirty-eight) would have to ratify any change. It therefore takes just thirteen states to block a constitutional amendment. The states with relatively few electoral votes have a strong interest in preserving the electoral college and its replication of the "Senate effect." Just as a small number of senators from the less populous states can effectively block legislation that most of the nation desires, so can a small number of those less populous states block a move away from presidential election by electoral vote and toward election by popular vote.

If we're not going to scrap the electoral college, then perhaps we could change two aspects of it. First, states could move from the current winner-take-all model to a model in which electoral votes are awarded in proportion to the popular vote in the state. The less populous states would still have their inflated number of electoral votes, but the allocation of those votes among candidates would be more representative of the candidates' strength at the polls. Second, even the states with relatively few electoral votes would probably agree that electoral votes should be locked in, not subject to the potential landmine of a faithless elector. Electoral votes should automatically accrue to the candidate who wins them. There is no need to run the risk that in a close election some party functionary who happens to be an elector might switch his or her vote and change the outcome of an election.

Part I. Counting by Hand

2. Manual Recounts

In Florida, and Across the Nation

On the morning after election day, it was clear that neither Bush nor Gore had the 270 electoral votes needed to become our forty-third president. Whoever would win Florida's twenty-five electoral votes would win the election, but that state was still too close to call. The focus of the postelection period in Florida became the battle over manual recounts of punch-card ballots. Bush led Gore after the initial statewide count, and again after a mandatory recount, but the election was not over, because Florida law permits a candidate to ask for manual recounts. Gore pushed for the hand counts, Bush opposed them, and the election ended when the U.S. Supreme Court held unconstitutional the Florida system for counting ballots by hand. Many of us watched on television as officials held punch-card ballots up to the light, scrutinizing the ballots for evidence of a voter's intent. To some of us it seemed perfectly understandable; to others, just downright odd. This chapter examines the purpose of manual recounts, discusses how officials try to figure out a voter's intent from looking at a ballot, and looks at some of the statutes and cases from around the country dealing with manual recounts.

First, some terminology. The phrases "hand count" and "manual count" are identical, and the phrases "hand recount" and "manual recount" are identical. If a county tallied ballots by hand on election night, without using a machine, that would be a hand or manual count. If a county used a machine first, and then counted ballots by hand afterward, that would be a hand or manual recount. And even those phrases are somewhat inaccurate. Although human hands are in fact picking up and sorting the ballots during a manual recount, the human eye plays the central role. Finally, here is the Webster's definition of the term "chad," a word heard often during the 2000 election: "[a] small piece[] of paper or cardboard produced in punching paper tape or punch cards."[1] In counties that use punch-card ballots, when the voter punches a hole in the ballot, the hole is created by pushing a little rectangular piece of cardboard out of the ballot. That little piece of cardboard is a chad.

Why have manual recounts? The simple answer is that the human eye can evaluate a ballot in a way that the machine eye cannot. The machine eye is a laser of light, looking for either a punched hole or a filled-in circle. In counties using punch-card ballots, the voter should punch a chad out of the punch-card for the candidate the voter prefers. When the cards are fed through the counting machine, the laser eye counts a vote if it sees a hole and doesn't count a vote if it doesn't see a hole. In counties using so-called optical scan ballots—the ones that look like SAT test forms—voters fill in little oval circles with a pencil. These ballots are also fed through counting machines, and here the laser eye is looking for a filled-in circle. If it sees one, it counts a vote; if it doesn't see one, it doesn't count a vote.

Manual recounts are helpful if, for whatever reason, the counting machines can't read all the ballots. One immediate response to this is: If a voter properly punches through a ballot card or properly marks an oval on a ballot card, then won't machines be completely accurate? In theory, yes. But the main purpose of manual recounting is not to ensure that properly punched and properly marked ballots are counted; they usually are. The main purpose of manual recounting is to ensure that improperly punched and improperly marked ballots are counted. States generally do not have laws providing that votes won't be counted if voters don't punch or mark ballots exactly right. Florida does not have such a law. Rather, states generally operate under a different principle: that every vote should be counted, if possible. So, although states try to educate voters to make sure their ballots are punched or marked correctly, votes are not automatically discarded if the ballots are improperly punched or marked.

Once one understands that voter error does not disqualify a ballot, the purpose of manual recounting is clear. Take two easy cases. Assume that a voter in a punch-card county punches a chad, but it does not fully detach. Assume it is hanging by one corner, detached at three corners. When that ballot is fed through the machine, the machine laser eye might not read the ballot as a vote. It might read the ballot as registering no vote for the office in question, here, the president. It would, in other words, record that ballot as an "undervote." A person who took that ballot and looked at it, however, could see that the voter intended to vote for a particular candidate—the candidate whose chad is almost fully detached. Similarly, assume that a voter in an optical-scan county fills in an oval incompletely, and assume, again, that the machine doesn't read the ballot as containing a vote. Here, too, the human eye could see that the voter intended to vote for the candidate whose oval was partially filled in.

So manual recounts can ensure that more votes are counted. They can ensure that voter error—or perhaps more charitably, incomplete punches or incomplete markings—does not sacrifice votes. Although the Bush team occasionally argued that only machines should count votes, that was never their main contention. Mostly they argued (a) that the Florida system for manual recounting is unconstitutional, and (b) that, while some incompletely punched ballots should be counted, others should not be.

On which ballots should chads count as evidence of a vote? A chad is "hanging" if it hangs onto the ballot by one of its corners and is detached at three corners. Here, the chad has clearly been punched but didn't detach fully. There was never much dispute about counting these ballots. They are clear evidence of a voter's intent.

A chad is "swinging" if it hangs onto the ballot by two corners and is detached at the other two corners. Here again, the chad has clearly been punched but didn't detach fully. There was never much dispute about counting these ballots, either. They, too, are clear evidence of a voter's intent.

A chad is called a "tri-chad" if it is attached to the ballot at three corners and has been detached at only one corner. Ballots containing these chads were disputed throughout. The Gore team wanted these counted as votes; the Bush team did not. Likewise, the two camps disputed whether to count ballots containing "dimpled" chads, otherwise called "indented" chads. These chads are not detached at all from the ballot. Although fully attached, they bear the impression of the voting tool (or "stylus"). Gore wanted ballots containing indented chads counted; Bush did not. Politically, the reasons were obvious. Bush, always ahead in the complete state count, feared that Gore would pick up a net gain of votes if ballots were counted by hand and would pick up an even larger net gain of votes if ballots with tri-chads and indented chads were counted. The reasons for this fear were (a) the manual recounting was occurring in majority Democratic counties, and (b) there is some evidence that Democratic voters failed to punch ballots fully more often than did Republican voters. Bush translated these political arguments into this question:

If the only evidence of a vote is a tri-chad or an indented chad, can we really be sure the voter intended to vote? One detached corner of a chad or the impression of the voting tool on a chad could mean an intent to vote but could just as easily mean the voter changed his mind or could merely be a stray marking on the ballot. We should count votes only when we are clear that they are votes, and not otherwise, argued Bush.

Gore responded that we must start from the presumption that when a voter takes the time to go to the polling place on a presidential election day, the voter intends to cast a vote for president. We have a high rate of citizens not voting at all; we shouldn't assume that those who show up at the polls don't mean to vote for president. If the ballot contained no evidence of a vote for president, or evidence of a vote for more than one candidate, then even Gore would back off. But so long as the ballot contained some evidence of a vote for one candidate—albeit slight evidence, such as a tri-chad or an indented chad—the presumption should favor counting that ballot as a vote, maintained Gore.

What does Florida law say? If Florida law said "count ballots containing indented chads" or if Florida law said "other than fully punched ballots, count ballots only if they contain hanging or swinging chads," much of the controversy would have disappeared. But Florida law is less clear. In the section specifically covering manual recounts, the law states only that officials should examine the ballot to determine "the voter's intent."[2] In a separate section of Florida law, officials are instructed to look for a "clear indication of the intent of the voter."[3] There is a difference between the two standards. Requiring "clear" evidence of voter intent is a higher evidentiary burden than requiring evidence of "voter intent," without the requirement that such evidence be "clear." This difference did not play much of a role, though, in the squabble over manual recounting in Florida. Furthermore, although Florida law empowers the secretary of state to issue regulations interpreting election law, there are no regulations interpreting either of these statutory provisions. Neither are there any Florida cases interpreting the meaning of "voter's intent" or "clear indication of the intent of the voter." The statutes give each county the power to recount ballots by hand, and, at various occasions throughout the postelection saga, Florida courts at different levels reiterated the statutory language, refusing to say anything more about how to ascertain the intent of the voter. What the courts all said, in one way or another, was that counties may not establish per se rules—they may not, that is, refuse to count certain chads or certain markings as evidence of a vote.[4] Rather, they must examine the totality of the circumstances—a legal fudge phrase meaning, "Look at all available evidence, but we won't tell you precisely what counts and what doesn't."

Thus, Florida law (a) sets forth a broad, vague standard, requiring an examination of ballots for evidence of voter intent, and (b) delegates that task to county officials. Bush challenged both aspects. He argued that the standard is too vague and that the discretion given to county officials is too subject to bias and inconsistent application. As discussed in chapter 9, a version of those arguments prevailed at the U.S. Supreme Court and helped end the election in Bush's favor. For now, though, it is helpful to see how the Florida standard for manual recounting compares with that used in other states. As it turns out, Florida is not unique. Many state statutes authorize manual recounts, and almost all do so without specifying clear rules for counting. Moreover, many judicial decisions have approved counting ballots on the basis of all sorts of evidence of voter intent.

In addition to Florida, statutes in the following states authorize manual recounts without specifying a standard for counting ballots: California, Indiana, Kentucky, Massachusetts, Minnesota,

Missouri, Montana, Nebraska, Nevada, New Jersey, Oklahoma, Pennsylvania, Rhode Island, South Dakota, Washington, and West Virginia.[5] That is a fairly broad array of states, from different geographic regions, of different sizes, and with different demographic makeups. In all these states, manual recounts are a standard part of elections practice. Some of these states make clear that manual recounts are the best way to ensure an accurate count. For example, Montana law provides that recount boards may "order manual counting of the votes cast if they believe it is necessary to resolve all questions relating to the election."[6] In Nebraska, if an initial machine recount reveals a substantial change from the initial count, "the ballots shall then be manually counted in any precinct which might reflect a substantial change."[7] Nevada insists on a manual recount for all ballots for an office if an initial partial recount reveals a significant discrepancy from the original machine count.[8] In Rhode Island, if an initial recount results in a margin of less than 3 percent between the winner and the second-place finisher, the losing candidate has a right to a manual recount of all ballots.[9] In Washington, a manual recount is also required (unless both candidates waive it) for close elections.[10] West Virginia requires a complete manual recount if the result of an initial sample manual recount is significantly different from the initial machine count.[11]

Thus, it is clear that manual recounts are part of elections practice in many states. But states generally do not provide guidance for counting ballots by hand. When officials are examining ballots, they are looking for what the voter did on the ballot, for evidence of the voter's preference. But precisely what should count as evidence of voter intent, and what should not count? Before examining how various state courts have dealt with this problem, it may be helpful to look at the one state that provides specific guidance for manually recounting punch-card ballots. It is, ironically, Texas.

George W. Bush, as governor of Texas, signed into law the one statute that gives clear guidance on counting ballots by hand. Here is what it says:

> (d) Subject to Subsection (e), in any manual count conducted under this code, a vote on a ballot on which a voter indicates a vote by punching a hole in the ballot may not be counted unless:
>   (1) at least two corners of the chad are detached;
>   (2) light is visible through the hole;
>   (3) an indentation on the chad from the stylus or other object is present and indicates a clearly ascertainable intent of the voter to vote; or
>   (4) the chad reflects by other means a clearly ascertainable intent of the voter to vote.
> (e) Subsection (d) does not supersede any clearly ascertainable intent of the voter.[12]

These subsections apply both to initial counting by hand and to manual recounting, which is the preferred method of recounting under Texas law.[13] The Texas statute sets out a general standard similar to that in Florida: "[C]learly ascertainable intent of the voter" is the basic rule officials must follow. But, unlike Florida, Texas gives statutory guidance. It lists at least three ways a ballot should be counted as a vote. Item (1) covers both swinging chads (two corners detached) and hanging chads (three corners detached). Item (2) covers ballots that have been punctured enough so that light is visible through the hole. Item (3) covers indented, that is, "dimpled," chads. If the Texas statute had been in effect in Florida, the Bush team could not have argued that the standard was too vague or that counties were applying different rules. If the Texas statute had been in effect in Florida, many more ballots would have been counted as votes, rather than rejected as undervotes. It is not clear whether Gore would have picked up enough net votes to prevail. But the entire course of the postelection period would have been different. Indeed, the argument on which Bush eventually prevailed at the U.S. Supreme Court—that the Florida standard was too vague and subject to inconsistent discretion of various county officials—would have disappeared. But Florida isn't Texas, and despite the ironic fact that the most specific hand-counting statute in the nation was signed into law by George W. Bush, that fact could be used only as effective rhetoric against Bush, not as binding law. The clear-intent-of-the-voter standard, although present in both Texas and Florida law, is not further defined in Florida, as it is in Texas. That proved to be a big difference.

Courts in many states have allowed voter intent to be discerned in a variety of ways. An early-twentieth-century Florida Supreme Court decision held that ascertaining voter intent is more important than strict adherence to instructions:

> While the general election law of the state directs that the X mark of the voter be made "before" the object of the elector's choice, there has been no authoritative holding here that the provisions requiring the X mark to be placed before the words voted on is mandatory, and that if the X mark is placed after the words voted on, the ballot should be discarded. . . . Where a ballot is so marked as to plainly indicate the voter's choice and intent in placing his marks thereon, it should be counted as marked unless some positive provision of law would be thereby violated.[14]

The Gore legal team frequently cited a Massachusetts high court decision, which included helpful language about dimpled, or indented, chads:

The critical question in this case is whether a discernible in-dentation made on or near a chad should be recorded as a vote for the person to whom the chad is assigned. The trial judge concluded that a vote should be recorded for a candidate if the chad was not removed but an impression was made on or near it. We agree with this conclusion. . . .

We find unpersuasive [the] contention that many voters started to express a preference in the congressional contest, made an impression on a punch card, but pulled the stylus back because they really did not want to express a choice on that contest. The large number of ballots with discernible impressions makes such an inference unwarranted, especially in a hotly contested election.

It is, of course, true that a voter who failed to push a stylus through the ballot and thereby create a hole in it could have done a better job of expressing his or her intent. Such a voter should not automatically be disqualified, however, like a litigant or one seeking favors from the government, because he or she failed to comply strictly with announced procedures. The voters are the owners of the government, and our rule that we seek to discern the voter's intention and to give it effect reflects the proper relation between government and those to whom it is responsible.[15]

In a second Massachusetts case, the state's high court again upheld a trial judge's use of a nonrestrictive standard:

[T]he judge correctly considered the character and location of the mark and the conditions attendant upon the election. In addition, the judge correctly inspected each ballot for patterns that reveal voters' intent. By focusing on a variety of factors, the judge was able to ascertain the intent of some voters whose ballots would have been treated as blanks under the light standard [which was more restrictive].[16]

An Illinois Supreme Court decision described the following problem with punch-card voting in an election for the state legislature:

> In some instances, the chad did not completely detach from the ballot, but the voter instead punctured a round hole in the chad, partially dislodged the chad or made a strong indentation in the chad. . . . [S]uch perforations and indentations may occur if a voter punches the ballot while it is outside the device, punches the ballot which is not properly attached to the four corners of the device, or, because of feebleness, does not apply the stylus to the ballot with sufficient force to dislodge the chad.[17]

The court refused to apply a strict rule, stating instead, "Nothing in our Election Code . . . requires voters to completely dislodge the chad from the ballot before their vote will be counted."[18] The court added:

> The purpose of our election laws is to obtain a correct expression of the intent of the voters. Our courts have repeatedly held that, where the intention of the voter can be ascertained with reasonable certainty from the ballot, that intention will be given effect even though the ballot is not strictly in conformity with the law. . . . The voters here did everything which the Election Code requires when they punched the appropriate chad with the stylus. These voters should not be disenfranchised where their intent may be ascertained with reasonable certainty, simply because the chad they punched did not completely dislodge from the ballot. Such a failure may be attributable to the fault of the election authorities, for failing to provide properly perforated paper, or it may be the result of the voter's disability or inadvertence. Whatever the reason, where the intention of the voter can be

fairly and satisfactorily ascertained, that intention should be given effect.[19]

The Connecticut Supreme Court evaluated manually recounted optical-scan ballots in a race for the U.S. Congress. One candidate argued that ballots should be counted only if voters had strictly complied with instructions on how to mark the ballot. The other candidate maintained that discerning the intent of the voter is paramount, "in light of all of the available evidence disclosed by the ballot."[20] The court agreed with the second candidate:

> [V]oting and counting votes mean, respectively, expressing intent and tabulating those expressions of intent in accordance with the legal principles governing those processes. Whatever the process used to vote and to count votes, differences in technology should not furnish a basis for disregarding the bedrock principle that the purpose of the voting process is to ascertain the intent of the voters.[21]

The court added:

> [W]e have long adhered to the principle that ballots should, where reasonably possible, be read so as to effectuate the expressed intent of the voter, so as not unreasonably to disenfranchise him or her. . . . Unless a ballot comes clearly within the prohibition of some statute it should be counted, if from it the wish or will of the voter can be ascertained.[22]

Other states have followed suit. The Alaska Supreme Court allowed the following manually examined ballots to be counted: "Boxes completely filled in over prior mark" (optical scan ballots); "Punch card ballots marked with a pen or pencil rather than being punched"; "Punch card ballots marked in pen or pencil and then punched in the same square"; and "Punch card ballots punched both immediately above the first square in a list of candidates and in the first square of the list of candidates."[23]

The Indiana Supreme Court offered this brief assessment of hanging chads:

> The trial judge found that since they did show that the square was punched out of the card, and the intention of the voter could clearly be discerned, it was proper to count these two votes. We see no reason to disturb the judgment of the trial judge in this regard. This is not a situation such as the one . . . above, where the ballot card did not show a punch mark or indentation.[24]

An Oklahoma Supreme Court decision made clear that checking the accuracy of counting machines is not what recounts are all about:

> We find that the recount in this case was misdirected in its focus. Its aim appears to have been an assessment of the accuracy of the electronic counting devices, and while we do not discount the importance of that inquiry, we find it to be secondary. The primary concern of an election recount, whether conducted by hand or by machine, is to find the will of the voters, as truly and faithfully as possible.[25]

Finally, the South Dakota Supreme Court stated a broad standard for manual counting:

> [A] vote shall be counted if the voter's intent is sufficiently plain and only if it is impossible to determine the voter's choice, shall any ballot or part thereof be void and not counted. . . .

It is not the policy of the State of South Dakota to disenfranchise its citizens of their constitutional right to vote. . . . Only if it is impossible to determine the voter's intent is a part of a ballot void and not counted. We presume every marking found where a vote should be to be an intended vote unless the contrary is clear.[26]

These cases and statutes from across the country make clear that Florida is not alone in permitting manual recounts. Machines are helpful in ensuring speed, and they achieve a certain degree of accuracy, but in close elections, many states prefer to count ballots the old-fashioned way, with the human eye. Although that fact is clear, the Bush team effectively obscured it for most of the postelection period. From early on, former Secretary of State James Baker suggested that hand counting was a dangerous business, and the Democrats never effectively dispelled that notion. Manual recounts did, though, remain at center stage.

3. Protesting the Election

What Sort of Deadline Was November 14?

Although nearly six million votes were cast in Florida, election-night returns showed that Bush led Gore by only 1,784 votes. Florida law requires an automatic machine recount if a candidate is ahead by "one-half of a percent or less of the votes cast for" the office in question.[1] In this case, that meant a mandatory recount if the margin of victory was 30,000 votes or less. So Florida conducted a statewide machine recount, which left Bush ahead by 300 votes. As permitted under Florida law, Gore then requested manual recounts in four counties: Broward, Miami-Dade, Palm Beach, and Volusia. Each granted the request, but it soon became apparent that they might not be able to complete the counting by November 14, a date that—arguably—was a firm deadline by which counties had to submit final vote totals. This chapter explains the Florida law on manual recounts, the arguments over whether November 14 was in fact a strict deadline, and the Florida Supreme Court's resolution of the dispute.

Manual recounts are not hard to get under Florida law. First, there is the question of who can request a manual recount and what the request must contain. Here is what the law says:

Any candidate whose name appeared on the ballot . . . or any political party whose candidates' names appeared on the ballot may file a written request with the county canvassing board for a manual recount. The written request shall contain a statement of the reason the manual recount is being requested.[2]

Note three things here. First, a candidate or a political party may request a manual recount. Second, voters have no such right. This omission led to a federal lawsuit, in which voters in a county not recounted by hand argued that their vote was at greater risk of not being counted than if they lived in one of the counties in which hand recounts were occurring. Third, although one must give a reason for a manual recount, the statute doesn't limit the type of reason that one may give. It is open-ended. How, then, must the county canvassing board respond? This, too, is open-ended. The law simply says that the "county canvassing board may authorize a manual recount."[3] Nothing more is said, so it is clear that the county canvassing board has broad discretion to determine what is an adequate reason for a recount request.

Each of Florida's sixty-seven counties submits its election returns to the state through the county canvassing board. The board is "composed of the supervisor of elections; a county court judge, who shall act as chair; and the chair of the board of county commissioners."[4] Normally, the board's role is to collect the election returns from the various precincts (by noon the day after the election[5]) and to file the returns with the secretary of state (who is the state's chief elections officer) by 5 P.M. one week after the election.[6] But, in the case of manual recount requests, the board has more to do.

If the board grants a request for a manual recount, it need examine only a small fraction of the county's votes. The law is very specific on this point:

The manual recount must include at least three precincts and at least 1 percent of the total votes cast for such candidate. . . . In the event there are less than three precincts involved in the election, all precincts shall be counted. The person who requested the recount shall choose three precincts to be recounted, and, if other precincts are recounted, the county canvassing board shall select the additional precincts.[7]

The Republicans continuously criticized Gore for seeking manual recounts in heavily Democratic counties and for selecting heavily Democratic precincts in those counties for the initial manual recount. Whether or not that criticism was justified from a political perspective, Gore was doing what Florida law allows. It allows candidates to request recounts in selected counties and to choose precincts within those counties.

In each of the four counties requested, the initial manual recount revealed vote totals different from those provided by the machine recount. One reason for this is that in some cases the human eye can see that a ballot contains a vote for president even though the machine laser "eye" cannot. In each of the four counties, Gore then requested a full countywide manual recount. The law here gives the county boards some options:

If the manual recount indicates an error in the vote tabulation which could affect the outcome of the election, the county canvassing board shall:
   (a) Correct the error and recount the remaining precincts with the vote tabulation system;
   (b) Request the Department of State to verify the tabulation software; or
   (c) Manually recount all ballots.[8]

So manually recounting all ballots is one option, and it is the option each of the four counties eventually chose. But, to get there, the county first needs to see whether the initial, limited recount indicates "an error in the vote tabulation which could affect the outcome of the election." This language led to a legal battle, pitting Secretary of State Katherine Harris (a Republican) against Attorney General Bob Butterworth (a Democrat).

In response to a request from the Palm Beach County canvassing board for interpretive help, Harris stated that "error in the vote tabulation" means there is something wrong with the hardware or software used to count the ballots. Butterworth then opined that "error in the vote tabulation" covers either a machinery problem or, even if the machinery is working just fine, a situation in which the machines fail to read votes that the human eye could read in the initial recount. The difference mattered. In three of the four counties in question, there was nothing wrong with the machines. (Volusia County had experienced some machine-related problems.) If Harris was correct, then the manual counting would have to stop with the initial, limited recount and could not proceed to the countywide level. The Florida Supreme Court ultimately sided unanimously with Butterworth. The statute says "error in the vote tabulation" and not "error in the vote tabulation system," and the Florida legislature elsewhere in the same statute used the phrases "vote tabulation system" and "automatic tabulating equipment" when it wanted to refer to "the voting system rather than the vote count."[9] This is a standard move in judicial interpretation of statutes. If a statute uses a particular phrase in one place and omits that phrase elsewhere, courts often infer that the legislature did not intend to use the phrase in both places.[10]

In each county, the initial manual recount had revealed vote totals that varied from the machine recount. Each county determined, accordingly, that the initial manual recount indicated an "error in the vote tabulation" (following the Butterworth interpretation later validated by the Florida high court), and each county opted to recount manually all the ballots in the county. Volusia County moved swiftly and completed its countywide recount by 5 P.M. on Tuesday, November 14, the statutory deadline for submitting final vote totals, or so Bush argued. The recount resulted in a net gain of ninety-eight votes for Gore. Palm Beach County voted to proceed with a countywide manual recount but delayed, in part because of the Harris opinion letter saying that no countywide manual recount was authorized because there was no machinery failure. Even after Butterworth issued his opinion letter, Palm Beach followed advice of counsel and waited until the Harris-Butterworth dispute was resolved in court. So there was no chance Palm Beach County would finish (let alone begin) its countywide manual recount by November 14. Broward County voted not to proceed with a countywide manual recount, largely on the basis of the Harris interpretation of "error in the vote tabulation"; when the Butterworth opinion came out, contradicting Harris, Broward reversed itself and voted for a countywide manual recount. But that, also, could not be completed by November 14. Miami-Dade County went back and forth for weeks about whether to proceed with a countywide manual recount. It, too, was unable to complete the count by November 14.

Palm Beach and Volusia, which had decided prior to November 14 to conduct a countywide recount, faced a dilemma. On the one hand, two separate sections of Florida law state clearly that counties must submit their election returns to the secretary of state by 5 P.M. one week after the election, that is, November 14. On the other hand, the section of Florida law that gives candidates the right to ask for manual recounts (the "protest" section) authorizes county boards to opt for a countywide manual recount, and such a recount might extend beyond the fourteenth. So, after Harris stated that she would not accept vote totals after the fourteenth, both counties sued her in state court. The cases were argued on Monday, November 13, and on

Tuesday, November 14, Judge Terry Lewis issued a classic split-the-difference ruling. Bush and Harris wanted him to rule that no manual recounts could be submitted after the fourteenth; Gore and the counties wanted him to rule that manual recounts had to be accepted after the fourteenth. Lewis ruled instead that Harris "may ignore . . . late filed returns, but may not do so arbitrarily, rather, only by the proper exercise of discretion after consideration of all appropriate facts and circumstances."[11] All the counties submitted their returns to Harris by 5 P.M. on November 14, and that evening Harris stated that, pursuant to Judge Lewis's ruling, any county wishing to file amended returns based on manual recounts would have to explain its reason in a letter to her the next day. Those letters arrived, and Harris rejected each request. The counties once again sued, charging that Harris had abused the discretion Judge Lewis said she should exercise. On Friday, November 17, Judge Lewis ruled that Harris had not abused her discretion.[12]

The election was about to end, with Bush the winner. Harris had long indicated that she was waiting for overseas military absentee ballots to arrive—they had a separate deadline of ten days after the election, that is, Friday, November 17. Although Florida law requires absentee ballots to be received by 7 P.M. on the day of the election,[13] federal law provides more expansive rights for the military. In the 1980s, the federal government sued Florida for restricting those rights, and the case was resolved via an agreement (called a "consent decree") supervised by a federal court, in which Florida agreed to count overseas absentee ballots received "no later than 10 days from the date of the Federal election."[14] To implement this agreement, Florida promulgated an administrative regulation, requiring overseas absentee ballots to be either "postmarked or signed and dated no later than the date of the Federal election."[15] The failure of some counties to read the "or" in that sentence led to one of the postelection controversies. Some counties insisted, improperly, that the overseas ballots had to be postmarked by the date of the election, even though the regulation allows a nonpostmarked ballot if it is signed and dated by election day. Because members of the military need not pay for mailing, their mail often bears no postmark.

The counties reported their vote totals on November 14, with Bush still ahead, and everyone assumed that when the overseas military vote came in, Bush's lead would increase. (That turned out to be correct; the military vote bumped his lead to 930.) Gore had to get Florida's high court to reverse Judge Lewis and insist on the inclusion of vote tallies from countywide manual recounts. Late on Friday afternoon, November 17, the Florida Supreme Court agreed to take the case and hear arguments on Monday, November 20. And it did more. Knowing that Harris was prepared to certify the election for Bush the next day (Saturday, November 18, after the overseas military votes were tallied), it enjoined her—on its own motion—from certifying the election until further order of the court. In other words, it ordered her not to certify the election until the Gore appeal was resolved, and it did so not in response to a Gore request for an injunction but on its own. The Gore legal team was willing to let Harris certify the election on the eighteenth, for Gore could then have immediately challenged the certification through Florida's "contest" laws. If the Florida high court had not enjoined the certification, the Gore contest would have had more time, and perhaps more hand recounts would have been completed.

The case came to the Florida Supreme Court.[16] It decided the Harris-Butterworth dispute, as discussed earlier, easily. But it had a separate, difficult, question to resolve. Does Florida law (a) prohibit the secretary of state from accepting hand-count tallies received after November 14, (b) require her to accept such late-filed tallies, or (c) give her discretion over the matter, and, in that case, what are the rules for her exercise of that discretion? Recall that Judge Lewis had construed Florida law as granting Harris discretion, but he ruled in a brief opinion that she had not abused her discretion. He never explained precisely the contours of that discretion. The Florida Supreme Court went further, ruling unanimously that Harris had only narrow discretion to reject late-filed returns and that she had abused her discretion. Here is how it reached its conclusion that more hand counts must be accepted.

Florida law establishes a state elections canvassing commission, which consists of the governor, the secretary of state, and the director of the Division of Elections. Governor Jeb Bush recused himself and was replaced by Agriculture Commissioner Bob Crawford. The other two members of the commission were Secretary of State Harris and Elections Director Clay Richards. The law states that the commission "shall, as soon as the official results are compiled from all counties, certify the results of the election and determine and declare who has been elected for each office."[17] The law also says the following, which was central to Bush's case: "If the county returns are not received by the Department of State by 5 p.m. of the seventh day following an election, all missing counties shall be ignored, and the results shown by the returns on file shall be certified."[18] Hand counting after that 5 P.M., November 14 deadline, was too late, or so Bush argued. The problem for Bush was that other statutory provisions left room for doubt. One section, after reiterating that counties must file returns by 5 P.M. a week after the election, continues this way: "If the returns are not received by the department [of State] by the time specified, such returns may be ignored and the results on file at that time may be certified by the department."[19] This provision says late-filed returns "may" be ignored. The other provision says they "shall" be ignored. These two provisions are flatly inconsistent—"shall be ignored" requires the secretary of state to turn a blind eye to late-filed returns; "may be ignored" provides room for discretion. Gore needed the court to give "may" precedence over "shall."

And the court did so. First it said that when two sections of state law conflict, "the specific statute controls the general statute."[20] The "shall be ignored" language occurs near the end of a statutory section that is mostly about the makeup and role of the elections canvassing commission. The "may be ignored" language is part of a statutory section specifically titled "Deadline for submission of county returns to the Department of State; penalties."[21] Not only does it set forth a deadline and discretion to ignore late-filed returns, but it also sets a fine of $200 per county canvassing board member for each day returns are late. The reason for letting this provision trump the other one is an inference that the legislature was more sharply focused on the issue in the section specifically dealing with deadlines and penalties for late filing.

Second, the court said that, when two sections of state law conflict, "the more recently enacted statute controls the older statute."[22] The "may be ignored" statute is more recent and thus is better evidence of legislative intent, because one can infer that the more recent legislature wrote with the prior law in mind. Third, the court said that the $200 per day fine provision would be rendered meaningless if late-filed returns had to be ignored. Counties would have no reason to file late in that case, and thus the fines would never come into play. The establishment of a system of fines makes sense, said the court, only if a county might sometimes have reason to think late-filed returns may be accepted and the county board members are willing to risk a penalty to take the extra time.

In addition to the directly conflicting "may be ignored" language, the high court pointed to a section of Florida law that describes the "official return of the election" as the results from machine counts "to which has been added the return of write-in, absentee, and manually counted votes."[23] Gore argued that this was evidence that the "official return" differed from the returns sent by 5 P.M. on November 14 and that an official return could include manually counted votes. Bush responded that there is no difference between the official return and the one due by November 14 and that the reference to manually counted votes makes sense because some counties might finish their full hand recount by the fourteenth and other counties might include the numbers from the initial "one percent" hand recount in their tallies. The court agreed with Gore.

A third section of Florida law that helped Gore is the one that authorizes manual recounts. Section 166 of the election law gives candidates the right to "protest" election returns by requesting manual recounts. Although no explicit language in that section refers to a deadline for filing returns with the state, two aspects of section 166 played a key role in the high court's ruling. First of all, it would be odd for the legislature to have granted county canvassing boards the power to authorize countywide manual recounts if such recounts would be ignored if they went on past the one-week reporting deadline. This is especially true of large counties, which would have a hard time finishing such recounts within a week of the election. Bush responded that the way to square the authorization of manual recounts with a seven-day deadline is to require counties to reject requests for recounts if such recounts cannot be completed in time. Bush also pointed to the requirement that county boards "appoint as many counting teams of at least two electors as is necessary to manually recount the ballots."[24] Bush's was a plausible reading of the law. But Gore had a response to the Bush argument, and it carried the day.

The protest section provides that a request for a manual recount "must be filed with the canvassing board prior to the time the canvassing board certifies the results for the office being protested or within 72 hours after midnight of the date the election was held, whichever occurs later."[25] Both sides agreed the counties had to certify results to the secretary of state by 5 P.M. on November 14; the dispute was over whether tallies from hand recounts filed after that deadline had to be accepted, as well. A candidate may request a manual recount seventy-two hours after midnight of the date of the election—in 2000 that would have been midnight on Friday, November 10—or *prior to the time the canvassing board certifies the results for the office being protested,* whichever is later. If a county could certify its results as late as 5 P.M. on November 14, then a candidate could request a manual recount at 4:59 P.M. on that day, because that would still be "prior to" county certification. Why would the legislature allow an eleventh-hour request for hand recounts, only to insist in a separate statutory section—and then only by implication—that the recounts be rendered meaningless the next minute? The way to read the statute as a whole—another rule of statutory interpretation the court used—is to require counties to file returns by 5 P.M. on November 14 but to allow results from manual recounts to be included afterward.

So the court rejected the Bush argument that November 14 was a firm deadline. But neither did it accept the full extent of the Gore argument—that all hand recounts had to be accepted, no matter when submitted. Instead, the court adopted the intermediate position—that Harris had discretion to accept or reject late-filed hand recount tallies—and it set forth the proper scope of her discretion. The court held her discretion to be narrow; it relied on a state constitutional and statutory concern for including as many votes as possible. Because manual recounts often reveal votes that machines cannot pick up, such recounts should be excluded only to accommodate two specific concerns, one from Florida law and one from federal law. The state law concern was this: Once a candidate is certified the winner of an election in Florida, the losing candidate has a statutory right to contest the election. The court held that Harris could reject manual recount tallies submitted after November 14 if late filing would preclude an election contest. The federal law concern was that, in the context of presidential elections, certain special deadlines exist. Although the court didn't quote any federal statutory language, it did say that Harris could reject late-filed tallies if accepting them would preclude "Florida voters from participating fully in the federal electoral process."[26] Electors around the country were to meet on December 18 to cast their vote for president, and December 12 was the last day for judicial proceedings to be completed if a state's electors were to be immune from challenge in Congress.[27] The Florida high court ruled on November 21, and it considered either December 12 or December 18 the relevant federal deadline, but it didn't say which one. Thus, the court wanted to (a) allow hand recounts to continue, under its reading of the various provisions already discussed, (b) allow the loser at the end of those hand recounts sufficient time to contest the election, and (c) ensure that the protest phase was concluded by either December 12 or December 18 (and perhaps the contest phase, too, although the court wasn't clear on this point). Accordingly, the court ordered Harris to accept the results of manual recounts until 5 P.M. on Sunday, November 26. Although that date is not found in any statute, it represents the Florida Supreme Court's attempt at reconciling the state law authorizing manual recounts during the protest phase, the state law authorizing election contests, and the federal law electoral deadlines that are peculiar to presidential elections.

The Florida Supreme Court issued its ruling on Tuesday night, November 21. The three counties that were attempting to complete countywide hand counts—Broward, Miami-Dade, and Palm Beach—had just about five days left to meet the deadline of November 26. Thanksgiving was coming up in two days. Broward, it appeared, would finish. It was unclear what would happen in the other two counties, and it was unclear whether Bush would appeal to the U.S. Supreme Court and whether that Court would take the case. The next chapter discusses the events between November 21 and November 26, which led to Harris's certifying Bush the winner in Florida and Gore's contesting that certification. Chapter 8 discusses the U.S. Supreme Court's response to the Florida Supreme Court's November 21 ruling—a response that turned out to be more smoke than fire, with one important exception: In response to a request from the nation's high court, the Florida Supreme Court clarified its references to federal electoral deadlines in a way that proved fatal for Al Gore's candidacy.

4. Contesting the Election

What Does the Law Mean by "Rejection of Legal Votes"?

With the newly set deadline of Sunday, November 26, just five days away, three counties raced against the clock to complete their hand counts. Broward County, whose ballot counters and canvassing board worked on Thanksgiving, finished late Saturday, the twenty-fifth. Broward counted not just hanging and swinging chads—the detached chads that most agree count as clear evidence of a voter's intent—but also indented, or "dimpled," chads, which bear the impression of the voting tool but are not detached at all from the ballot. There are various ways of thinking about whether an indented chad is evidence of a voter's intent. Broward looked for corroborating evidence in a particular way. If a chad for (say) Gore was indented, and the voter otherwise voted a straight Democratic ticket, Broward counted the chad for Gore. It did the same thing on the Republican side. Although voters sometimes split their tickets, voting for some Democrats, some Republicans, Broward thought party-line voting was common enough to rely on it as corroborating evidence that an indented chad in the presidential race should be counted.

Palm Beach County, which all along had worked slowly, took Thanksgiving off. And by Sunday afternoon, it was clear Palm Beach would not finish its hand count by the 5 P.M. deadline. Palm Beach had been using a more restrictive standard than

Broward. Palm Beach would count an indented chad as evidence of a voter's intent only if that voter had indented chads in other races on the ballot. In other words, if the voter managed to press through the ballot card and remove the chad either entirely or partially in all the other races, then Palm Beach deemed it less likely that an isolated indented chad in the presidential race was evidence of an intent to vote. On the contrary, if the voter indented chads in the presidential race and at least one other race, that counted as evidence that the voter had difficulty breaking the chad with the voting tool but still intended to vote for the candidates whose chads were indented by the tool. In any event, Palm Beach did not finish by the 5 P.M., November 26 deadline. It asked Secretary of State Harris for an extension, which she denied. She would not accept a partial recount, either, so she certified the prior Palm Beach totals (the ones submitted on November 14).

Miami-Dade County had flip-flopped a few times on whether to conduct a countywide manual recount, but by Monday the twentieth it was proceeding, and by Tuesday night, when the Florida Supreme Court extended the counting until the twenty-sixth, it was one-fifth complete. But on Wednesday, the day before Thanksgiving, the Miami-Dade canvassing board made two decisions that might well have sealed Al Gore's fate. First, Miami-Dade decided it would not have enough time to recount the entire county by hand and meet the Sunday deadline. So it decided to recount just the "undervotes," that is, those ballots for which the machine registered no vote for president. But the Republicans protested that only a full countywide recount would be fair and legal. They seemed particularly concerned about full counting of heavily Republican, Cuban-American precincts. In addition, the GOP staged a loud, raucous protest, which nearly became violent. Perhaps in response—although the county canvassing board denied it—the board made its second decision. On

Wednesday afternoon, the board voted unanimously to stop the recount altogether. David Leahy, the county supervisor of elections, stated that the board had decided that a recount of just the undervotes was improper and that a full recount was impossible by the twenty-sixth. Gore sued to force Miami-Dade to resume the count, but a trial court, an appellate court, and the Florida Supreme Court all refused to order the count to resume. County canvassing boards have significant discretion under Florida law to grant or deny recounts, and, although that discretion had gone Gore's way for the initial two weeks after the election, in Miami-Dade the discretion was finally exercised against him.

Miami-Dade certified its numbers from the fourteenth. But the board revealed that, before the counting stopped, with one-fifth of the recount completed, Gore had gained a net of 168 votes. And, although Harris accepted Palm Beach's numbers only from the fourteenth, Palm Beach pressed on and completed its hand recount a few hours after the 5 P.M. deadline, revealing a net gain for Gore of 215. Broward, which was the only one of the three counties able to certify new tallies from a complete recount, yielded a net gain of 567 for Gore. During the five-day period between the Florida high court's ruling and the deadline on Sunday, November 26, some other counties had adjusted their tallies, as well, to account for failure to count certain overseas military ballots. Thus, when Harris announced the new vote totals on Sunday evening, Bush had a lead of 537. And that was enough. Harris certified that Bush had won the vote in Florida and had won Florida's electors. Governor Jeb Bush, pursuant to federal statute,[1] certified the vote as well, and the "certificate of ascertainment" was sent to Washington. Unless the certification was overturned, Florida's twenty-five electoral votes would be enough to give George W. Bush the White House.

□

The battle now moved to the contest phase. Under a Florida law amended in 1999, a losing candidate can sue to set aside the certified result of an election. The statute lists five grounds for such a lawsuit.[2] The first requires proof of "misconduct, fraud, or corruption," which Gore did not try to show. The second demands showing that the winner was ineligible for the office in question, also not at issue here. A third requires proof of bribery, and there was no proof of that. A fourth operates as a vague catch-all provision, allowing the loser to show that the winner wasn't "duly . . . elected," but Gore didn't rely on this either. Instead, he placed all his eggs in one basket and nearly won the election. Here is the statutory ground on which Gore contested the Bush victory: "Receipt of a number of illegal votes or rejection of a number of legal votes sufficient to change or place in doubt the result of the election."[3] Gore claimed that *illegal votes* had been *received* in only one county. Nassau County, he claimed, had submitted on the twenty-sixth its initial machine count from election night, rather than the mandatory machine recount, with a net gain for Bush of 51 votes. Gore lost this argument at trial and again on appeal.

But Gore had four separate claims that *legal votes* had been *rejected*. First, he argued that he had gained 215 net votes once Palm Beach completed its recount. To be sure, Harris had refused to accept that recount because it had not been completed by the 5 P.M., November 26 deadline established by the Florida Supreme Court. No matter, said Gore. That was the protest phase; this is the contest phase. And, although Harris may have been well within her power to stick to a protest-phase deadline, once a candidate is contesting another candidate's certification as the winner, all the loser need do is point to votes that went uncounted, even if no one did anything illegal in not counting them. Gore's was a literalist argument: "rejection of a number of legal votes" means what it appears to mean, and here Harris had rejected legal votes that would have yielded a net gain of 215 votes for Gore. The argument was literalist in another way, as well. Gore's claim was that the combination of the various votes that were rejected was enough to change or at the very least "place in doubt the result of the election."

The other three claims had a similar ring. The second was that Palm Beach had used too restrictive a standard in counting ballots. As discussed earlier, its standard was indeed more restrictive than the standard applied in Broward, which counted many more indented chads as votes than did Palm Beach. Gore argued that Palm Beach had refused to include 3,300 ballots (not all of them for Gore) in its vote tallies even though those ballots contained evidence of a vote for president. That refusal, said Gore, amounted to a rejection of legal votes. His third argument was that Miami-Dade had refused to certify the partial recount it had completed, which had yielded a net gain of 168 votes for Gore. That, too, he said, amounted to a rejection of legal votes. These first three arguments all involved rejection of legal votes by human beings—Harris had rejected the 215 net gain from Palm Beach, Palm Beach officials had rejected 3,300 ballots, Miami-Dade officials had rejected a 168 net gain. The fourth argument involved rejection of votes not by people but by a machine. Here Gore argued that in the four-fifths of Miami-Dade that was never recounted, the vote tabulating machine had identified about 9,000 ballots as containing no vote for president. In other words, the machine had rejected those votes. A hand count of those votes might reveal sufficient indicia of voters' intent to allow at least some of the ballots to be counted as a vote for president, rather than as a no-vote. So Gore demanded that such a count take place.

Bush's response revealed a totally different understanding of the contest section of Florida law. Once a winner is certified, Bush argued, such certification should generally be difficult to overturn, and the loser should have to show some form of illegality or abuse of discretion. Thus, when Harris followed the Florida high court's 5 P.M., November 26 deadline, she had done nothing illegal, and the net gain later revealed for Gore was properly rejected. In other words, Bush argued that it is not enough to show that votes were "rejected." The statute also requires a showing that the rejected votes were "legal" ones, and votes are not legal ones if they have been rejected according to law. The same argument carried over to Gore's other claims. Palm Beach, Bush argued, did not illegally reject the 3,300 ballots that it considered to contain insufficient evidence of voter's intent. Yes, it had rejected those votes, but it had not rejected "legal" votes because its determination that the votes were not legal ones was made according to law and at the very least did not represent an abuse of discretion. Miami-Dade, indeed, refused to certify a partial recount that would have yielded a net gain for Gore of 168 votes, but in rejecting those votes it did nothing illegal, since there is no provision in Florida law authorizing submission of a partial recount. Miami-Dade did not, in other words, reject "legal" votes. Or so Bush argued. Finally, although the machine in Miami-Dade revealed approximately 9,000 additional "undervotes"—and one could say it had rejected those votes—again, Bush maintained, there is no reason to call those "legal" votes, because the county canvassing board acted well within its discretionary powers in deciding to scrap the countywide recount entirely.

Bush buttressed his argument with a reference to the protest section of Florida law. That section grants discretion to county canvassing boards to decide whether to conduct an initial sample manual recount and then whether to conduct a follow-up countywide manual recount. Why would the legislature have given county boards such broad discretion if a losing candidate could, through a contest, demand that partial or late votes be counted and demand that a recount of undervotes occur even if the county had good reasons for saying No to such a re-count? Wouldn't Gore's reading of the contest statute render the protest phase less meaningful or perhaps (in the case of undervotes) irrelevant?

The difference between the Gore and the Bush positions was stark. Not only would adoption of the Gore position put him on the precipice of victory, but also any losing candidate in the future would be able to point to uncounted votes and get them counted at the contest phase. No court had ever interpreted the recently amended contest statute, so this would be a case of first impression. The presidency was hanging in the balance. Would the Florida courts adopt Gore's literal, seemingly simple reading of "rejection of legal votes," or would they adopt Bush's more contextual argument, relying on an understanding of the entire package of Florida election law provisions to require a showing that some official had acted illegally, not merely that votes remained to be counted? There was a deep irony about the arguments at this stage. At the earlier, protest phase, it was Bush who was advancing a literalist position and Gore who was the contextualist. Then, Bush had argued that a state statute literally required the secretary of state to ignore county returns submitted after November 14; Gore, in contrast, had argued that, when viewed in context of other statutory provisions, literalism must give way. Now, in the contest phase, Gore was relying on a literal reading of "rejection of legal votes," while Bush was insisting that such literalism made no sense in context of other provisions of Florida election law.

Gore filed his contest action on Monday, November 27, the day after Harris certified Bush the winner in Florida. The case was filed in trial court in the state capital of Tallahassee, as required by law, and it was assigned at random to Judge N. Sanders Sauls.

Judge Sauls compromised between Gore's desire for a very fast trial and Bush's desire for a slow one. He set the hearing for Saturday, December 2. During the intervening five days, Gore asked the Florida Supreme Court to expedite matters and to order prompt counting of the Miami-Dade undervote, but the high court denied his request. The trial got under way in Judge Sauls's courtroom, and it lasted two days.

It was not much of a trial. Gore's arguments never depended much on disputed issues of fact. Gore had gambled that his literal reading of "rejection of legal votes" would prevail and that he would win back rejected votes from Palm Beach and Miami-Dade and get the undervotes counted in Miami-Dade without having to show anyone had done anything illegal. But Gore did put on two witnesses. The first, an expert in voting systems, explained that punch-card machinery has various problems and thus that hand counting is often needed to ensure that votes don't slip between the cracks. The other witness, an expert statistician, explained that the rate of undervotes in counties using punch-card systems exceeded the rate of undervotes in counties using other voting systems, by a margin that could not be explained merely by chance and apparently not by demographics, either. Bush's witnesses sought to contradict the Gore witnesses, and some other Bush witnesses revealed that county officials had acted well within their discretion. But the big issue was not whose witnesses would be believed. The big issue was whether Judge Sauls would buy the basic Gore theory of "rejection of legal votes" or whether he would adopt the basic Bush theory requiring proof of illegality or abuse of discretion.

On Monday, December 4, Judge Sauls ruled for Bush in every possible way. First, Judge Sauls held that, to win an election contest, a plaintiff must show a "reasonable probability that the results of the election would have been changed."[4] The evidence presented, he held, failed to show such a reasonable probability.

Second, he held that Gore had failed to prove any illegality or abuse of discretion. Third, he held that, if a losing candidate wishes to contest a certain type of irregularity (for example, undervotes), the irregularity must be corrected across the state, not just in the county or counties selected by the plaintiff. In short, Judge Sauls rejected every argument raised by Gore and accepted every argument raised by Bush. Gore filed an immediate appeal, and the Florida Supreme Court held oral argument on Thursday, December 7.[5]

The court ruled quickly, on Friday afternoon, December 8. By the narrowest of margins, 4-3, the court reversed Judge Sauls and adopted the Gore position almost entirely. On the first holding from Judge Sauls, the high court held that his "reasonable probability" standard was based on outdated caselaw and that he had failed to account for the 1999 revision to the contest statute, which permits a losing candidate to argue that inclusion of rejected legal votes would "change or place in doubt the result of the election." On the second holding from Judge Sauls, the high court held that it was not necessary for a losing candidate to show illegality or abuse of discretion. Here was the key to the case. The Florida Supreme Court rejected the Bush position that an allegation of "rejection of legal votes" requires the plaintiff to show misbehavior on the part of an elections official. Instead, the court accepted the stark literalism of the Gore argument, and it ruled for him dramatically. It held that "rejection" of legal votes has the meaning Gore ascribed to it—either human beings or machines can be said to have rejected votes. And, relying on a different section of Florida law, it held that a vote is a "legal" one if there is a "clear indication of the intent of the voter."[6]

Based on these interpretations of Florida election law, the court ordered the 215 net gain for Gore from the late Palm

Beach recount back into the Gore column.[7] Harris had rejected those votes, but they were legal ones and should be included, said the court. It also ordered the 168 net gain for Gore from the partial Miami-Dade recount back into the Gore column. The Miami-Dade canvassing board had rejected those votes by refusing to certify a partial recount, but the court held that they were legal votes and should be included. The result of these two holdings was a net gain for Gore of 383, still not enough to prevail. The court also held, though, that Gore had a right to have the 9,000 undervotes counted in Miami-Dade. These, too, were legal votes that had been rejected, and Judge Sauls had not even examined those undervote ballots, even though they had been admitted into evidence and even though the law gives the court power to ensure that each allegation is "investigated, examined, or checked, to prevent or correct any alleged wrong."[8] Together, this package of 383 net gain votes for Gore, plus the possibility of more from the 9,000 Miami-Dade undervotes, was sufficient at least to "place in doubt the result of the election." Although the court affirmed Judge Sauls regarding Nassau County (it was allowed to submit its election-night totals, rather than its totals from the machine recount) and regarding the 3,300 Palm Beach ballots that Gore claimed had been counted too restrictively (those ballots would not be reexamined), it had nonetheless handed a stunning victory to Gore.

The court's ruling that a vote is legal if there is a "clear indication of the intent of the voter" demands further examination. The contest section of Florida law—the one invoked by Gore in this case, the one containing the "rejection of legal votes" rule—contains no standard for evaluating whether a ballot contains a legal vote. So the court looked elsewhere in the election code. The section of Florida law the court cited for its holding describes a process for hand-counting ballots that are "damaged or defective" and therefore "cannot be counted properly by the automatic tabulating equipment."[9] In such cases, the law says the ballots should be counted by hand and adds, "No vote shall be declared invalid or void if there is a clear indication of the intent of the voter as determined by the canvassing board."[10] Bush argued, unsuccessfully, that this "clear indication of the intent of the voter" standard applies only to the damaged or defective ballot circumstance and that it was inappropriate to import the standard into the counting of undervotes more generally. The "clear indication" standard is actually stricter than the other standard that the court could have deemed relevant. The protest section of Florida's election law refers to determining "a voter's intent" when counting by hand,[11] which is arguably an easier standard to meet than ascertaining a "clear indication" of a voter's intent.

Looking beyond the statutory section at issue (here, the contest section) to determine the meaning of a key term (here, "legal vote") is a common judicial maneuver. What remains a hard and important question is whether the court should have distinguished between what counts as the standard for determining voter intent and what counts as a "legal vote" for contesting a certified election. It is possible that a vote is not a legal one, even if, there is a clear indication of the intent of the voter, if, for some other, valid reason, the ballot was not counted. The Bush critique of the court on this crucial point is that various officials had perfectly legal, valid reasons for not counting certain votes— even on ballots where the voter's intent was clear—and thus that these counties had not rejected "legal" votes. In other words, Harris acted within the law by not accepting the Palm Beach recount that came in after the deadline set by the high court; Miami-Dade officials acted within the law by not certifying partial recount results, for state law does not authorize certification of partial results; and those same officials acted within the law by not conducting a countywide recount, for such a recount is not mandated by Florida law. This critique of the Florida Supreme

Court was Bush's strongest, namely, that the court improperly interpreted what the law means by "legal" vote.

Yet, as already discussed, the court adopted the very different reading of "rejection of legal votes"—any rejection by an official or a machine of ballots for which there is a clear indication of the intent of the voter—and turned to crafting a remedy. In issuing its remedial order, the court went further than Gore had requested, somewhat ironically supporting Judge Sauls's third holding, requiring that any irregularity be corrected statewide. The contest section of Florida law gives courts power to "provide any relief appropriate under [the] circumstances."[12] The court ruled that not only would the 9,000 Miami-Dade undervotes be recounted; so, too, should all undervotes throughout the state be examined by hand, to ensure that, where there is clear evidence of voter intent, such votes be included in the final tallies. This aspect of the ruling helped to ward off one aspect of a constitutional challenge to the Florida hand counting that had never been fully resolved in the courts. The argument is that, unless manual recounts are conducted statewide, voters in some counties will have greater opportunity to ensure that their votes are included than will voters in other counties. The Florida Supreme Court's statewide remedy held this argument at bay. All of the new counting—of the Miami-Dade undervotes and the rest of the statewide undervotes—was to begin "immediately."[13]

Chief Justice Wells wrote a scathing dissent. (Six of the Florida Supreme Court justices, including Chief Justice Wells, were identified as registered Democrats. One, Justice Harding, was identified as an independent.) Courts must defer to county officials unless the officials act illegally or abuse their discretion, said Wells. Furthermore, the most recent Florida case involving election contests (although decided prior to the 1999 revision to the contest statute) requires a showing of "substantial noncompliance with statutory election procedures,"[14] which had not been shown here, Wells maintained. Procedures for manual recounts are set forth in the protest statute, not in the contest statute, and the protest statute sets forth the county canvassing boards' role. The Gore position, said Wells, was fundamentally unsound, for it required a counting of the undervotes "upon the mere filing of a contest," without any showing that "enough legal votes were rejected to place in doubt the results of the election," which we cannot know until the undervotes are counted.[15] This catch-22, said Wells, works against Gore's position, not in favor of it. Moreover, argued Wells, by ordering counting resumed, the majority failed to take into account the upcoming federal electoral college deadlines and failed to specify procedures for the statewide count of undervotes. Finally, the standard for ascertaining a voter's intent was, in Wells's view, "constitutionally suspect."[16]

Justice Harding filed a separate dissent, joined by Justice Shaw. Harding agreed with the majority that Judge Sauls had erred by requiring a "reasonable probability that the results of the election would have been changed" and erred by requiring Gore to prove that the county canvassing boards had acted illegally or had abused their discretion. But Harding nonetheless voted to affirm the trial judge. Harding reasoned that Gore had failed to submit adequate evidence that, in a statewide recount of the undervote, the outcome would "likely be changed."[17] It was a much narrower dissent than that penned by Chief Justice Wells.

So the matter was remanded to the trial court, and almost instantaneously Judge Sauls recused himself, indicating only that he had "good and sufficient cause."[18] The case was reassigned to Judge Lewis, who had earlier ruled in Bush's favor during the protest phase, when he held that Secretary of State Harris had not abused her discretion in refusing to accept hand-count tallies submitted after November 14. The Florida Supreme Court had reversed Lewis at the protest phase, but the matter was now back before him at the contest phase. He had to supervise the newly ordered recounts. After an extraordinary late-night hearing, Lewis ruled that his fellow judges in Tallahassee would supervise the hand counting of the 9,000 Miami-Dade undervotes, which were sitting in a vault, never examined by Judge Sauls. The counting would begin early the next day, Saturday, December 9. Furthermore, Judge Lewis instructed county canvassing boards throughout the state to begin their manual recounts of the undervotes as soon as possible and declared that all the counting be completed by 2 P.M. on Sunday, December 10. It was a tall order, and, although counting began in earnest early Saturday, it was never finished. For, on Saturday afternoon, the U.S. Supreme Court, responding to a request from Bush, issued a stay of the Florida Supreme Court's ruling and took his appeal, setting oral argument for Monday, two days hence. The hand counting stopped, and it never resumed. Chapter 9 explores the stay order, as well as the ultimate ruling of the nation's high court that ended the election. Before discussing that final ruling, however, it is necessary first to review, in chapter 5, the last piece of the puzzle concerning counting by hand and then to explore, in chapters 6 through 8, the other key part of the Bush challenge to what was happening in Florida, namely that the Florida Supreme Court was legislating rather than interpreting and was thereby usurping the powers of the Florida legislature.

5. Challenging Hand Counts in Federal Court

The Seed Is Planted

Soon after it became clear that Florida would determine the outcome of the 2000 presidential election, the parties' strategies diverged. Gore, behind in the vote by a slim margin, sought to use Florida's statutory provisions for manual recounts to rescue ballots that the machines couldn't read but that perhaps a human eye could. Bush, ahead narrowly, wanted to stop all counting. So, as Gore proceeded to file for manual recounts in four counties, Bush was first into court, seeking to stop, or "enjoin," those recounts. This chapter discusses the Republican lawsuits brought in federal district court (the first, or trial court level) and traces those lawsuits through their final resting point in the federal court of appeals. Although the lawsuits discussed in this chapter were not the ones that ultimately won the election for Bush, they set the stage for the case that closed out the election in the U.S. Supreme Court.

The lawsuits were a joint venture of the Bush legal team and Republican residents of Florida counties in which Gore had not asked for manual recounts. The argument raised primarily by Bush was that the standard for assessing ballots by hand, or, more accurately, by the human eye, is too vague. Florida law authorizes county canvassing boards to scrutinize a ballot for evidence of a voter's intent. On some ballots that will, of course, be an easy task. If all ballots in a county are recounted by hand, most will have one and only one chad completely detached in the race for president. That is the candidate for whom the voter intended to vote. Other ballots will have two chads detached, and, under Florida law, those "double-punched" ballots (also known as "over-votes") may not be counted.[1] The debate was always over a third set of ballots, the so-called undervotes. These are the ballots that the machines read as having no vote for president. Upon human inspection, some undervotes indeed bear no evidence of a vote for president. But others clearly reveal a vote that the machine could not read. The examples both Bush and Gore agreed upon were hanging or swinging chads. As discussed in chapter 2, hanging chads are detached at three corners and are hanging by one, while swinging chads are detached at two corners and are hanging by the other two. Machines often cannot read these ballots because the machine laser eye sees a piece of the chad and thinks the ballot-card has not been punched. The human eye can see that the voter didn't fully detach the chad but clearly intended to vote for a particular candidate. And, even though voters are instructed to inspect their ballot-cards before placing them in the box, nothing in Florida law renders invalid ballots that have evidence of a vote even if the chad is not fully detached. In fact, county canvassing boards are instructed to look, during a manual recount, for a voter's intent.

Bush's concern was with the so-called tri-chads (detached at one corner only) and the so-called dimpled or indented chads (those that are not detached but that contain an impression made by the voting tool). Bush argued (a) that the voter's intent standard is too vague to have clear application to these types of chad, (b) that different counties had different interpretations of a voter's intent, some counting tri-chads, some not, some counting dimpled chads, some not, (c) that different counties counted dimpled chads differently, and (d) that the standards were uncertain and constantly shifting. To bring the case in federal court, as Bush did, he needed to convert these concerns into a matter of federal law, so he argued that the Florida manual recount system violated the federal constitutional guarantees of due process and equal protection. The due process concern focused on the vagueness of "voter's intent" as a standard. Any vote-counting process under a statutory standard such as "voter's intent" would be changeable and arbitrary, argued Bush. The equal protection argument took the due process argument one step further, to the point of application in the different counties. Bush maintained that each voter in Florida has a right to have his or her vote counted according to a common standard, that the "voter's intent" standard on its face (that is, as written in the law) provides no assurance that votes would be counted similarly across counties, and that there was evidence that the standard was already being inconsistently applied. The problem for Bush's argument —and it is a problem that never really went away, in the minds of many, even though a version of the equal protection argument ultimately prevailed at the U.S. Supreme Court—is that there is a similar inequality in virtually every aspect of how we elect a president, but no court has ever thought the system unconstitutional. That is, states use different voting methods, and within some states there are different methods, as well. Punch-card ballots, optical scan ballots, paper ballots, machines with levers—these are all used in Florida, for example, and they all have different rates of error in counting votes. Certainly this is a kind of inequality, and arguably it harmed Gore more than Bush, for there is evidence that the rate of machine error is highest in punch-card counties, where Gore generally outpolled Bush.

In any event, Bush had set forth a plausible federal claim. The other Republican plaintiffs, residents of counties not being recounted by hand, offered a different type of equal protection argument. They contended that their votes were at greater risk of never being registered in the vote tallies than were the votes of residents in counties where ballots were being recounted by hand. The factual claim seems indisputable. Undervotes can be read by the human eye and added to vote tallies only if the human eye is given a chance to look. That chance was occurring in the four counties in which Gore had asked for manual recounts but not elsewhere. The hard question was not factual but legal. Did the GOP voter plaintiffs state a good equal protection argument, or were they merely griping? The main Gore response to their claim was that Bush had the same right under Florida law as Gore to request manual recounts in whichever counties he wished. If Bush instead chose to challenge the constitutionality of those recounts, his voters shouldn't be permitted to adopt a different strategy in federal court. But the GOP voters responded that it was their rights, not Bush's, that were at stake. They maintained that Bush's strategic choice not to seek recounts in other counties shouldn't prevent residents of those counties from raising concerns that their votes had a reduced chance of being counted. One aspect of the GOP voters' lawsuit was never really clarified, though. When one brings an equal protection argument of the sort they were bringing, two different remedies are possible. One requires counting undervotes in all counties (that would make things equal). The other requires counting undervotes in no counties (that would also make things equal). It seems as though the GOP voters desired the latter remedy, but a court that ruled in their favor could have ordered the former, instead. Indeed, when the Florida Supreme Court ruled for Gore in his election contest, it ordered a statewide count of the undervote, thereby warding off an equal protection argument like the one raised by the GOP voters in their federal court lawsuit.

□

So there were basically two claims on the table—the "voter's intent" standard was too vague and therefore subject to inconsistent application, and counting by hand in some but not all counties harmed those voters in counties not being recounted by hand. Bush and the GOP plaintiffs were seeking an injunction against hand counting, however, and thus they faced two legal hurdles. First, they needed to convince the federal district judge, Donald M. Middlebrooks, that they were likely to prevail on the merits of their claims at a full trial. Second, they needed to convince him that they would be irreparably harmed if he didn't stop the hand counting. Proof of irreparable injury was necessary because plaintiffs were asking for a preliminary injunction, in advance of a full trial, and courts do not enjoin government officials in the "preliminary" posture unless it is clear that plaintiffs are suffering or will suffer a harm that cannot be fixed later on. Judge Middlebrooks ruled against Bush and the GOP voter plaintiffs both on the merits and on the irreparable injury issue.

Judge Middlebrooks first rejected plaintiffs' arguments on the merits. After describing the Florida system for manual recounts, he deemed it "reasonable and nondiscriminatory on its face."[2] He stated that, as written, the system favors neither party, and it helps achieve a more accurate count. Additionally, Middlebrooks recognized that state legislatures have broad latitude in establishing election procedures, in presidential as well as in state elections. "[F]ederal courts should tread cautiously," he wrote, "in the traditional state province of electoral procedures and tabulations."[3] As to the core of plaintiffs' arguments—the failure of the statutes to provide clear rules for assessing voter intent during manual recounts and the possibility that hand recounts would not take place in some counties—Middlebrooks concluded that these problems are "unavoidable given the inherent decentralization involved in state electoral and state recount procedures."[4] He then sang the praises of decentralization:

> Rather than a sign of weakness or constitutional injury, some solace can be taken in the fact that no one centralized body or person can control the tabulation of an entire statewide or national election. For the more county boards and individuals involved in the electoral regulation process, the less likely it becomes that corruption, bias or error can influence the ultimate result of an election.[5]

Middlebrooks also pointed out that manual recounts are used across the country and have been used since the founding of the nation. No type of vote tabulation is free from error, he added, and "the very premise of a manual recount after an electronic tabulation . . . is to provide an additional check on the accuracy of the ballot count."[6]

Turning to the question of irreparable injury, Judge Middlebrooks noted that manual recounts were just under way in the four counties in question and that there was not yet proof of constitutional problems. Pointing to the "contest" statute that Gore eventually used, Middlebrooks stated that Florida law provides candidates state court opportunities to challenge election results. Finally, rejecting a theory of irreparable harm that Justice Scalia was later to embrace, Middlebrooks once again turned away the Bush lawsuit:

> The mere possibility that the eventual result of the challenged manual recounts will be to envelop the president-elect in a cloud of illegitimacy does not justify enjoining the current manual recount processes under way. Central to our democratic process, as well as to our Constitution, is the belief that open and transparent government, whenever possible, best

serves the public interest. Nowhere can the public dissemination of truth be more vital than in the election procedures for determining the next presidency.[7]

Two groups of GOP voters had filed suit, raising equal protection claims. One group was part of the Bush lawsuit, resolved by Judge Middlebrooks. Another group filed a separate lawsuit. The federal judge hearing that separate case, Judge John Antoon II, rejected plaintiffs' request for an order to stop the hand counting, basing his ruling on Judge Middlebrooks's opinion in the related case, which had been issued the day before.[8] All of the losing plaintiffs, from both lower court cases, asked the federal court of appeals with jurisdiction over the matter—the Eleventh Circuit, which sits in Atlanta—to issue an injunction against the hand counting pending their appeal of Judge Middlebrooks's ruling. Usually federal appeals courts resolve cases through three-judge panels, but an appeals courts can sit "en banc"—that is, all the judges in that circuit participate—for matters of great importance. Accordingly, the Eleventh Circuit considered en banc the motions for an injunction pending appeal. In an unsigned order without dissent, the full court—all twelve judges—denied the motions. The opinion explained that "the state courts will address and resolve any necessary federal constitutional issues presented to them."[9] Therefore, intervention of the federal courts was unnecessary, at least at that moment. There was no harm that could not be repaired either through the state court process or, if the state courts addressed the federal constitutional claims inadequately, through later proceedings in the federal courts.

Although the motion for an injunction pending appeal had been denied, the appeals from Judge Middlebrooks's and Judge Antoon's rulings sat before the Eleventh Circuit, waiting to be argued. In an unusual move, the losing side from the Middlebrooks decision—Bush and some of the GOP voters—petitioned the U.S. Supreme Court for a "writ of certiorari before judgment." A writ of certiorari is the fancy phrase for what the Supreme Court does when it decides to hear an appeal—it grants a petition for a writ of certiorari. What was unusual was asking the Supreme Court to intervene before the federal court of appeals had ruled. The merits arguments in the petition were familiar from the trial court stage. Allowing counties to use different counting rules violates the equal protection clause; allowing manual recounts in some counties but not in others violates the equal protection clause, as well; and the statutory failure to set a clear common standard violates the due process clause. The petitioners added a twist. They argued that Florida law violated the First Amendment by giving the county canvassing boards unconstrained discretion over manual recounts. The Supreme Court denied the petition for a writ of certiorari before judgment, and the case remained in the federal court of appeals.

The Eleventh Circuit heard oral arguments in both appeals en banc and issued its rulings on Wednesday, December 6. At that time, Bush had already been certified the winner in Florida, Gore had lost his contest action in Judge Sauls's trial court, and Gore's appeal from that ruling was pending before the Florida Supreme Court. Manual recounts had halted. It did not look like a dire situation for Bush. The case for irreparable injury looked fairly weak. So it was not a big surprise that eight of the twelve judges on the Eleventh Circuit joined two unsigned "per curiam" opinions ("for the court") affirming the trial judges' orders denying plaintiffs' request for an injunction. The court concluded that there was no current irreparable injury to Bush or to any of the individual plaintiffs who were claiming their votes were at unequal risk of not being counted. The court did not resolve the merits of the plaintiffs' arguments.

On the irreparable injury issue, the court wrote that Bush and vice president candidate Dick Cheney

> are suffering no serious harm, let alone irreparable harm, because they have been certified as the winners of Florida's electoral votes notwithstanding the inclusion of manually recounted ballots. Moreover, even if manual recounts were to resume pursuant to a state court order, it is wholly speculative as to whether the results of those recounts may eventually place Vice President Gore ahead.[10]

Similarly, the court held that the individual plaintiffs had not shown immediate injury and had not shown any injury that could not be remedied through standard court proceedings; that is, they had not shown the need for the kind of immediate relief that a preliminary injunction offers.

Four of the twelve Eleventh Circuit judges dissented, and their dissents were vigorous. Judge Tjoflat wrote a long dissent, joined by Judges Birch, Dubina, and Carnes (who joined in part). Judge Tjoflat pointed out that only some counties were being recounted by hand and that different counting standards were being used in different counties. The Florida Supreme Court had interpreted the Florida system for election "protests" as permitting a county canvassing board to authorize hand recounts not just for machine error but also for any vote tabulation error, and candidates were likely to ask for hand recounts in counties, and precincts within counties, where they thought it likely they would pick up votes. Judge Tjoflat described this selectivity as "cherry-pick[ing]" and described the possibility of counting dimpled chads in some counties only as the "selective dimple model."[11] Judge Tjoflat also noted that Florida law authorizes county canvassing boards to proceed to a countywide manual recount only if the initial 1 percent recount reveals an "error in the vote tabulation which could affect the outcome of the election."[12] The candidate ahead in the vote could never receive a countywide manual recount, reasoned Judge Tjoflat, because correcting an error in his favor would only increase his lead, not "affect the outcome of the election."

From these observations, Judge Tjoflat drew two conclusions. First, he argued that the Florida Supreme Court's ruling permitting countywide manual recounts even absent problems with machines constituted an unconstitutional change in Florida law. In other words, Judge Tjoflat agreed with Secretary of State Harris and not with Attorney General Butterworth (and not with the unanimous Florida Supreme Court, which had sided with Butterworth) on the question of when a countywide manual recount is properly triggered. It is highly unusual for federal judges to issue opinions disagreeing with state courts on matters of state law. An important early-twentieth-century U.S. Supreme Court decision made clear that federal courts are to defer to state court interpretations of state law.[13] There might be a small window for federal judicial involvement in the setting of presidential elections if state courts in fact rewrite state law, rather than interpret it. The theory behind this—that in the setting of presidential elections special constitutional rules govern the relationship between state legislatures and state courts—is explored in chapters 6 through 8. But the Florida Supreme Court's ruling on when a countywide manual recount may be triggered was a standard example of judicial interpretation of a statute, not judicial legislation. In short, even if a federal court disagrees with a state court's interpretation of state law, it is not the place of the federal court to displace that interpretation. That is a cardinal rule of our federalism, our system that divides power between the federal and state governments.

Perhaps recognizing the weakness of his first argument, Judge Tjoflat reached his second and more strongly reasoned conclusion. He argued that, because manual recounts might take place in some counties only, the equal protection rights of voters in other counties are violated. Voters are discriminated against based on their county of residence. Additionally, Judge Tjoflat maintained that because the candidate trailing in the race (here, Gore) had asked for recounts only in counties that otherwise favored him, the Florida system encouraged selectivity based on party affiliation, another equal protection violation. Finally, Judge Tjoflat contended that the equal protection harm to the individual voters constituted irreparable injury, and he refused to accept the possibility that those voters could seek redress through contest actions after a winner was certified. Florida law permits individual voters to contest an election, but Judge Tjoflat reasoned that, because their candidate had prevailed at the certification stage, the Bush voters would be unable to show that rejection of their votes would change or place in doubt the outcome of the election, as required by Florida law. At most, they could argue that extra Bush votes would add to the Bush lead, but that isn't a ground for a contest. One might respond that, if Bush were the winner, then how would Bush voters be harmed? Their answer, and Judge Tjoflat's, is that the harm would arise from unequal counting, even if their preferred candidate prevails.

Judge Carnes also wrote a long dissent, joined by Judges Tjoflat, Birch, and Dubina. He focused on the selectivity of manual recounts in certain counties only and reasoned that the equal protection rights of voters in other counties were being violated. He accepted "as a fact for present purposes the proposition that manual recounts of punch card ballots will result in intended votes being counted that otherwise would not have been if the process had stopped with machine tabulation."[14] Given that assumption (an assumption that Judge Carnes stated was the basic position of the Democrats), voters in counties not recounted by hand had a smaller chance than voters in counties recounted by hand of ensuring that their votes would be accurately counted. That amounts to an inequality of voting rights that raises equal protection concerns, reasoned Judge Carnes.

Judge Birch also wrote a dissent, joined by Judges Tjoflat and Dubina. He focused on the vagueness of the "voter's intent" standard and the concern that such a standard would be implemented "based only upon the disparate and unguided subjective opinion of a partisan (two members are elected in partisan voting) canvassing board."[15] Judge Dubina also wrote a brief dissent, joined by Judges Tjoflat and Birch.

Although the majority per curiam opinions (for eight judges) addressed only the irreparable injury issue, Chief Judge Anderson wrote separately to respond to the dissenters on the merits. On the issue of recounts in some counties but not others, Chief Judge Anderson argued that "greater certainty in some counties than in others that every voter's intent is effectuated"[16] does not amount to an equal protection violation. "Taking this argument to its logical conclusion," reasoned Chief Judge Anderson, "would lead to the untenable position that the method of casting and counting votes would have to be identical in all states and in every county of each state."[17] Furthermore, Florida law provides various safeguards against unfair counting, including having a county judge on each county canvassing board, requiring open county canvassing board meetings, and providing for judicial review of a board's decisions. Additionally, all candidates and political parties have a statutory right to request recounts in any county. Judge Anderson also echoed Judge Middlebrooks's praise for the decentralization of Florida's election system. Finally, he concluded that insufficient evidence existed, at least at the time, to show that the "voter's intent" standard was being applied in a constitutionally inconsistent manner across counties.

"Voter's intent," although not precise, is nonetheless a standard (i.e., the statute doesn't say "count as you like"), and various procedural safeguards, such as openness of the counting and judicial review, protect against manipulation.

Although the Eleventh Circuit ruled against Bush and the GOP voters, the dissents raised serious questions about the Florida system for manual recounts. As discussed in chapter 4, the argument based on recounting in some counties but not others was put to rest by the Florida Supreme Court's order of a statewide manual recount of undervotes, in response to Gore's election contest. But the argument that "voter's intent" is a vague standard subject to differential application across counties never went away. Indeed, as explored in chapter 9, it became the centerpiece of the U.S. Supreme Court's ultimate ruling in favor of Bush.

Part II. The Bush Attack on the Florida Supreme Court

6. The "Safe-Harbor" Provision and Article II of the Constitution

Did the Florida Supreme Court Rewrite Florida Law?

The Florida Supreme Court twice ruled for Gore. The first time, as described in chapter 3, it allowed manual recounts to continue past the November 14 statutory deadline for counties to certify vote totals to the secretary of state. The new deadline was November 26, set by the court in an effort to accommodate manual recounts, election contests under state law, and the federal electoral college timetable. After Bush was certified the winner on November 26, Gore contested that certification and eventually prevailed again at the Florida Supreme Court, as explained in chapter 4.

After both losses in the Florida Supreme Court, Bush appealed to the U.S. Supreme Court. Both times the nation's high court took the appeal; both times it set aside the Florida high court's rulings. Chapter 9 discusses in detail the final blow from the U.S. Supreme Court—the decision that ended the election by holding unconstitutional the Florida manual recount system. This chapter and the next two explore Bush's first appeal, from Gore's victory at the protest stage.

When the Florida Supreme Court unanimously allowed hand counting to continue until November 26, Bush went to the U.S.

Supreme Court with three arguments, or questions presented, as arguments to the nation's high court are called. The Court granted his appeal only as to two and added a third question of its own. Bush's first question was whether the Florida Supreme Court had violated 3 U.S.C. § 5, which is a section of federal law dealing with how states resolve electoral-vote challenges. His second question was whether the Florida Supreme Court had violated Article II of the federal Constitution, which grants to state legislatures the power to determine the manner of appointing electors. The Court's third question was what should happen if it ruled for Bush on the 3 U.S.C. § 5 issue. (Interestingly, the Bush question that the Court did not take up was whether the manual counting system in Florida violated the Constitution. That was the issue on which the Court ultimately ended the election, in Bush's second appeal.)

The first Bush question dealt with 3 U.S.C. § 5, which became known as the "safe-harbor" provision. Here is its text:

> If any State shall have provided, by laws enacted prior to the day fixed for the appointment of the electors, for its final determination of any controversy or contest concerning the appointment of all or any of the electors of such State, by judicial or other methods or procedures, and such determination shall have been made at least six days prior to the time fixed for the meeting of the electors, such determination . . . shall be conclusive, and shall govern in the counting of the electoral votes as provided in the Constitution. . . .[1]

This is a classic piece of legal complexity, but it can be pulled apart and put back together. Section 5 was enacted in response to the Hayes-Tilden election of 1876. That election involved disputed electoral slates from three states and was resolved via an ad hoc commission put together by Congress amid much political horse-trading. To avoid future chaos, Congress, in 1887, passed the Electoral Count Act. Part of that Act establishes rules for Congress if states present conflicting slates of electors. Section 5 was another important aspect of the Electoral Count Act. It gives states an incentive to (a) have in place a method for resolving electoral controversies and (b) get those controversies resolved in a timely fashion.

In 2000, the electors were to meet on December 18, in state capitals across the country, as provided by federal law.[2] So the relevant date under Section 5 was December 12—if a state could resolve any electoral controversy no later than that date ("six days prior to the time fixed for the meeting of electors"), it could ensure against a fight over its electors. That is so because Section 5 deems any slate determined by judicial methods to be "conclusive" if the judicial proceedings are completed no later than the key date—in 2000, December 12. That date became known as the "safe-harbor" date, for if a state could wrap things up no later than that date, its electors would be like a boat in a safe harbor, protected from stormy seas. In other words, the electors would be protected against the threat of a competing slate of electors presenting itself as the legally chosen slate.

But, to gain the protection of the safe harbor, judicial contests must be resolved under "laws enacted prior to the day fixed for the appointment of electors [i.e., election day]." This is not a complex legal rule. It denies safe-harbor protection if a state relies on what is commonly called "retroactive" lawmaking. One can think of an easy example. If by election day a state had enacted no legislation to resolve contests over electors, and if after election day it enacted such a law, applying that law to the current controversy would not satisfy Section 5's requirement of "laws enacted prior to" election day.

Bush's first question presented to the U.S. Supreme Court in his protest-stage appeal was whether the Florida Supreme Court had changed Florida law after election day, thereby depriving Florida of the chance to take advantage of the safe harbor. If one could prove that the Florida Supreme Court had changed the law in existence as of election day, thereby depriving the state of the possibility of the safe-harbor protection, then one could argue that Section 5 had been violated. There would, however, be a knotty question of the sort lawyers call "ripeness"—is there yet an injury? For it was never clear exactly how Bush was being injured by the prospective possibility of the loss of Florida's safe harbor. To be sure, he might be hurt down the road—if a Bush slate of electors somehow had to face a challenge from a Gore slate of electors, and if such a challenge could have been prevented by proper invocation of the safe-harbor provision. But precisely how Bush was being hurt in advance of such a scenario was never clear. Moreover, Section 5 is a conditional, rather than an absolute, section of federal law. If the Florida Supreme Court rewrote law and thereby deprived the state of the safe-harbor opportunity, arguably Section 5 would just drop out of the picture. If the "if" isn't met, then the "then" can't follow. This doesn't look like a violation of the law. On the other hand, perhaps depriving the state's citizens of the opportunity to take advantage of the safe harbor, and to ward off any electoral challenges, would itself have been a violation of federal law.

Did the Florida Supreme Court change the law that existed on election day? This issue, as it turns out, is the same as the one presented in Bush's second question to the U.S. Supreme Court, although it came up in a somewhat different manner. When the framers of the Constitution established the electoral college system, they left much to state legislatures, via the following constitutional language: "Each State shall appoint, in such manner as the legislature thereof may direct, a number of electors, equal to the whole number of Senators and Representatives to which the State may be entitled in the Congress."[3] It is not disputed that this language grants substantial power to state legislatures. For example, state legislatures may choose the electors themselves (this used to be common), or they may delegate that power to the people of the state (this is now done across the nation). They may award all electors to the state's popular vote winner (this is the practice in forty-eight states and in the District of Columbia), or they may parcel out electors according to districts or vote percentage (some version of this is now in place in two states).

The second question Bush presented to the U.S. Supreme Court in his appeal at the protest stage was whether the Florida Supreme Court had rewritten Florida law, thereby usurping the powers constitutionally granted to the Florida legislature to determine the "manner" for appointing (i.e., choosing) electors. Bush's two questions presented were, thus, really one question, with two possible legal violations. Had the Florida Supreme Court rewritten the law? If it had, then it arguably had violated the safe-harbor provision of federal law, and it also had violated the federal constitutional prerogatives of the Florida legislature.

But Bush's arguments that the Florida Supreme Court had rewritten Florida law were weak and never gained majority support on the U.S. Supreme Court. To understand this, it is important, first, to see the difference between the role of state courts and the role of federal courts when interpreting state law. Generally, federal courts decide only questions of federal law—interpretations of the U.S. Constitution or federal statutes, regulations, or treaties. There are times, though, that federal courts are faced with questions of state law, either because those questions come packaged with federal law questions or because the federal courts are hearing a so-called diversity case—one in which a citizen of one state sues a citizen of another state, creating "diversity" of state citizenship between the parties. Those suits can be brought in state court, but the Constitution gives jurisdiction to federal courts to hear them, as well. Sometimes plaintiffs bring diversity cases in federal court. Sometimes defendants "remove" to federal court diversity cases brought by plaintiffs in state court. When a federal court must decide a question of state law, it looks to the state courts to see how they have resolved or would likely resolve the question. This rule of deference to state-court interpretation of state law is the result of a landmark U.S. Supreme Court decision from early in the twentieth century referred to now as the "*Erie* doctrine."[4] It is a bedrock principle of the division of power between the federal and state governments.

Thus, if the U.S. Supreme Court simply disagreed with the Florida Supreme Court about how to interpret Florida law, that would be no ground for reversal. The U.S. Supreme Court is not supreme regarding the interpretation of Florida law. The Florida Supreme Court is. The question whether the Florida Supreme Court had misinterpreted Florida election law during the protest phase by extending the deadline for manual recounts to November 26 was not a question of federal law; as a question of state law, it was not something the U.S. Supreme Court had any power to decide. The only way, therefore, for Bush to have a chance at overturning the state court decision was to persuade the U.S. Supreme Court that the Florida Supreme Court had done more than interpret. If the Florida high court had in fact legislated— if it had rewritten Florida law, snatching power away from the Florida legislature—then Bush could argue that Article II of the Constitution and (perhaps) the safe-harbor provision had been violated.

There are obvious examples of a state court rewriting state law. If state law says that electoral votes go to the candidate who receives the most votes (as Florida law says) and a state court says that electoral votes go to the second-place candidate, that is an obvious rewriting of state law. If state law says there may never be a manual recount and a state court says there may be a manual recount, that, too, is an obvious rewriting of state law. And, germane to this case, if state law says November 14 is the last day on which counties may submit vote totals and a state court extends that deadline, that is a rewriting of state law. This, of course, was precisely Bush's argument. Bush argued that state law required the secretary of state to ignore election returns filed after November 14. The Florida Supreme Court's decision permitting the results of manual recounts to be filed as late as November 26, maintained Bush, constituted a rewriting of Florida law and, accordingly, was a violation of federal law and the federal Constitution.

The problem with this argument was that Florida law doesn't just contain the provision dictating that the secretary of state "shall" ignore returns filed after November 14. There are other provisions of Florida law that come into play, and those provisions also must be examined and interpreted by the Florida courts. As explored in chapter 3, the relevant parts of Florida law are:

(a) The section of law saying that the secretary of state "may" ignore returns filed after November 14. "May" and "shall" are different words, and the Florida Supreme Court needed to sort out the contradiction. Using standard tools of statutory interpretation, the Florida high court determined that "may" rather than "shall" governs.

(b) The section of law authorizing countywide manual recounts and permitting initial recounts to be requested any time prior to the time for counties to certify election results. The Florida Supreme Court reasoned that the legislature wouldn't have written this section—the "protest" section— if it intended it to become immediately moot, and thereby the court interpreted the secretary of state's discretion to ignore returns filed after November 14 in light of the need to complete countywide manual recounts authorized by the protest section.

(c) The section of law granting a candidate who loses after statewide certification the right to contest that loss in court, plus the sections of federal law setting electoral college deadlines. The Florida Supreme Court, after interpreting conflicting state law provisions to mean that manual recount tallies should be accepted past November 14, also had to ensure that a losing candidate could bring an election contest (state law), while ensuring adherence to the electoral college timetable (federal law). Neither the Florida legislature nor the U.S. Congress had clearly addressed this problem, so the court did what courts always do—it crafted a remedy to resolve a statutory mess.

The point, again, is not whether one agrees with the Florida Supreme Court's decision as an interpretive matter. Perhaps there were other ways of reading Florida law. The point is that the Florida high court was engaged in *interpretation*, trying to make sense of statutory provisions that don't fit together well. For Bush to prevail, he needed to show that the Florida Supreme Court had crossed the line from interpretation to legislation. To do that, he needed to show that there was no reasonable basis for the Florida high court's interpretation and thus that the purported interpretation was really law-writing. But the Florida Supreme Court's decision during the protest phase was clearly an effort at construing varying sections of state law (in light of some federal deadlines). This was not a case in which a state court flatly contradicted a legislative statement without a basis for doing so in other statutory provisions.

Thus, the Florida Supreme Court did not usurp the prerogatives of the Florida legislature. Consistent with the safe-harbor provision of federal law, the Florida high court relied on "laws enacted prior to the day fixed for the appointment of the electors." Consistent with Article II of the federal Constitution, the Florida high court did not interfere with the Florida legislature's power to determine the "manner" by which electors are selected. The U.S. Supreme Court never ruled in Gore's favor on these issues, but neither did it rule in Bush's favor. Chapter 8 discusses how the U.S. Supreme Court instead sent the protest-stage case back to the Florida Supreme Court for clarification and examines how the Florida high court responded. But, first, chapter 7 covers another aspect of the attack on the Florida Supreme Court.

7. Article II of the U.S. Constitution

Did the Florida Supreme Court Improperly Rely on the Florida Constitution?

Bush's arguments that the Florida Supreme Court legislated rather than interpreted were weak. He could not convincingly show that the Florida high court had rewritten Florida law, thereby sacrificing the state's opportunity to gain the protection of the safe-harbor provision and usurping the federal constitutional prerogatives of the Florida legislature. These arguments never prevailed.

Perhaps sensing that those arguments would not persuade a majority of his colleagues, Justice Scalia came up with something during oral argument in Bush's first appeal, from the protest-stage victory for Gore at the Florida Supreme Court, that the Bush lawyers had only briefly mentioned. Justice Scalia asked Gore's attorney, Professor Laurence Tribe, whether (a) the U.S. Constitution grants state legislatures precedence over state constitutions in the setting of presidential elections and (b) whether the Florida Supreme Court had violated that rule by placing the Florida Constitution above statutes passed by the Florida legislature.

The structure of this argument is odd. Normally, constitutions take precedence over statutes. Indeed, one of the primary purposes of constitutions is to create higher, or supreme, law and thereby to limit the lawmaking powers of legislatures and the administrative powers of executives. The U.S. Constitution states that it (and laws made pursuant to it) is the supreme law of the land.[1] The U.S. Supreme Court, beginning in 1803 with *Marbury v. Madison*,[2] has explained that the Constitution trumps federal and state law if the law is inconsistent with the Constitution.

State constitutions operate in similar fashion. Although they cannot take precedence over the federal Constitution or federal law, they do trump state statutes. That is, if a state legislature passes a law preventing citizens from "doing X," and the state constitution gives citizens a right to "do X," then the state law must give way to the state constitution. That is why we have constitutions—to limit our transient legislative needs in the light of higher principle. There was no dispute between the parties about this basic relationship between constitutions and statutes.

What was odd about Scalia's line of questioning was that it inverted the normal order of things. It suggested that, in the setting of presidential elections, in the event of an inconsistency between a state constitution and a state law, the state constitution must give way. This chapter first examines the source of this suggestion and then turns to whether the Florida Supreme Court indeed violated a rule of legislative, rather than constitutional, supremacy in the presidential election setting.

The source of Scalia's questioning is the grant of power to state legislatures in Article II of the federal Constitution: "Each State shall appoint, in such manner as the legislature thereof may direct, a number of electors, equal to the whole number of Senators and Representatives to which the State may be entitled in the Congress." Because the Constitution expressly delegates to state legislatures the power to determine the "manner" of selecting electors, that delegation must be interpreted as flipping the usual supremacy of state constitutions, or so Scalia suggested.

This is a plausible, but not certain, textual argument. Demanding that state constitutions give way to state legislatures is a dramatic inversion of the normal power structure, and perhaps the framers of the Constitution would have spoken more clearly had they desired this outcome. That is, they could have written not only the language just quoted, but also an additional phrase. For example, after "in such manner as the legislature thereof may direct," the framers could have added, "notwithstanding any arguably inconsistent provision of a State's constitution." Courts often demand that legislatures (or constitution framers) speak clearly when displacing a standard principle of law.

Although there is no clear statement of the framers' intent to place state legislatures above state constitutions in the setting of presidential elections, Scalia's argument was nonetheless based in the constitutional text giving state legislatures the power to determine the "manner" of choosing electors. And he had some caselaw on his side, as well: an 1892 Court decision, *McPherson v. Blacker.*[3] The facts of *McPherson* are unlike those of the 2000 election, but some of the *McPherson* Court's discussion is relevant. The issue in *McPherson* was whether the Michigan legislature could allocate presidential electors by district, rather than across the state as a whole. Plaintiffs' main argument was that the state is one entity and may not be divided. The Court responded in two easy moves. First, the federal Constitution grants power to states to determine how electors are chosen, and states operate through whatever political bodies are set up under state constitutions. If the Michigan constitution grants power to the legislature, and the legislature through law provides for electoral districts, then the people of Michigan have spoken. There is no overarching principle that a state must act as a whole unit. Second, the U.S. Constitution is even more specific than this, for it grants to state legislatures the power to determine the manner for choosing electors. This language can't be seen as limiting state legislative power.

All of that makes complete sense, but none of it says that state constitutions must give way to state statutes. There is one passage in *McPherson*, though, that supports Scalia's interpretation. Here is the language:

> [I]f the words "in such manner as the legislature thereof may direct" had been omitted, it would seem that the legislative power of appointment could not have been successfully questioned in the absence of any provision in the state constitution in that regard. Hence the insertion of those words, *while operating as a limitation upon the State in respect of any attempt to circumscribe the legislative power,* cannot be held to operate as a limitation on that power itself.[4]

This is not wonderfully clear writing, and this passage is "dicta," not necessary for resolution of the case, but its meaning can be teased out. The Court is saying that the federal constitutional power granted to state legislatures limits a state's attempt at circumscribing the legislature's power. How would a state attempt to do so? Through its constitution, of course. (Perhaps also through its governor. One could imagine a situation in which a state's executive seeks to determine the choosing of electors in a way that saps power from the state legislature.) The language emphasized in the excerpt, although not clearly addressing the issue of when a constitution must give way to a legislative enactment, does say that "any attempt" by a state at limiting the legislature's power in the setting of presidential elections is limited by the grant of power to state legislatures in Article II of the U.S. Constitution.[5]

There are three problems with this understanding of the constitutional grant of power to state legislatures. The first, as discussed earlier, is that the framers could have been clearer about making state statutes supreme over state constitutions. Second, the political structure of a state government—its organization into executive, legislative, and judicial branches—is the creature of that state's constitution, just as the federal structure of government is the product of the federal Constitution. How can a state's constitution yield to a state's legislature, if the legislature can operate only pursuant to state constitutional norms? State constitutions, after all, determine how state legislatures are elected and what procedures are necessary for the passage of legislation.

Third, the better reading of *McPherson*—and of the Article II delegation of power to state legislatures to determine the manner of choosing presidential electors—is that the state legislature is supreme in its specific choices regarding federal presidential elections, but not in its more general election law provisions that apply across the board to presidential elections, congressional elections, and state and local elections. In other words, a state constitution may not insist, for example, on popular vote for electors, or winner-take-all for electors, if the state legislature wants to appoint electors itself or through districts. But if the state legislature writes a general elections code, and that code applies to all elections held in the state, that code is still subject to state constitutional rules. All of the Florida statutory provisions that the state courts had to interpret in resolving the 2000 election were general provisions of this sort. There was never a claim that the courts had elevated a state constitutional provision over a state legislative choice specifically directed to choosing presidential electors.

These arguments aside, Scalia's question was on the table. He was concerned that the Florida Supreme Court had relied on the state's constitution to displace statutory choices made by the state legislature, in violation of the Article II delegation of power to state legislatures. A close examination of the Florida Supreme

Court's opinion reveals that Scalia was only partly correct. When it resolved the basic conflicts in Florida statutes—"may" versus "shall" and the relevance of the section authorizing manual recounts—the Florida high court did not rely on the state constitution. Only after explaining that the secretary of state could not automatically reject election returns filed after November 14 did the court turn to the state constitution for guidance in determining the secretary's proper scope of discretion. It relied on state constitutional provisions concerning the right to vote and concluded that the secretary's discretion to ignore manual recount numbers after November 14 was limited. It then looked again at statutes and concluded that the secretary could reject manual recount tallies only if accepting those tallies past a certain date would (a) take away a losing candidate's opportunity to contest the election, under state law, or (b) jeopardize the state's ability to comply with federal electoral college deadlines. Even if any invocation of a state constitution in the setting of a presidential election is invalid, the Florida Supreme Court's protest-stage ruling would have been invalid only in its reliance on the constitutional right to vote in limiting the secretary's scope of discretion. But the court had statutes to rely on, as well, and perhaps that would have been enough. Perhaps the court could have written the same opinion without relying on the state constitution. Indeed, as discussed in the next chapter, the Florida Supreme Court revised its opinion on remand from the U.S. Supreme Court and relied on statutory analysis without using the state constitution.

8. The U.S. Supreme Court Asks for Clarification

The Florida Supreme Court Responds

After Gore won his protest-stage case at the Florida Supreme Court, Bush appealed to the United States Supreme Court. As described in chapter 3, the state court had rejected Bush's argument that all counting must cease on November 14 and had granted Gore's request for an extended timetable for manual recounting of ballots. The state court issued its ruling on Tuesday, November 21, and set a new deadline of Sunday, November 26. The U.S. Supreme Court granted Bush's appeal on Friday, November 24, and set oral arguments for the following Friday, December 1. In between, although hand counting continued in two counties, Gore still trailed, and Secretary of State Harris certified the election for Bush on November 26. Gore began his contest proceeding, challenging that certification.

Bush could have withdrawn his appeal to the U.S. high court. After all, he was now the presumptive winner, and it was no longer clear how he was injured by Gore's protest-stage victory at the state high court. To be sure, that victory gave Gore extra days for hand counting, and the Bush margin of victory on the twenty-sixth was less than it otherwise might have been. But Bush was still ahead, and if Gore were to win his contest and eventually come out ahead in the vote tallies, then Bush could file one big appeal at the U.S. Supreme Court, combining his protest-stage and contest-stage arguments. Bush also ran a risk in pushing forward with his appeal. If the U.S. Supreme Court were to rule for Gore, such a ruling would legitimize the process taking place in Florida, in the courts and in the counties if new counts were ordered. Such a ruling—a federal seal of approval—would greatly increase the pressure on Bush to concede if Gore were to come out ahead in the vote tallies.

Despite these reasons for withdrawing his appeal, Bush did not, and the case came to the nation's high court. Although Bush had asked the Court to consider three issues, it accepted the appeal only on two, and, as discussed in chapter 6, both boiled down to one question: Had the Florida Supreme Court legislated, rather than interpreted, thereby usurping the prerogatives of the Florida Legislature? If so, then arguably both federal law and the federal Constitution had been violated. (The Court also asked a question of its own: "What would be the consequences of this Court's finding that the decision of the Supreme Court of Florida does not comply with 3 U.S.C. Sec. 5?")[1]

In his brief to the Court, Bush first argued that the Florida Supreme Court's judgment did not comply with the safe-harbor provision, 3 U.S.C. § 5. The safe-harbor provision grants immunity from challenge to a state's electoral slate if (a) judicial contests are completed no later than December 12 and (b) they are completed pursuant to law in existence as of election day. Bush's argument was that the Florida Supreme Court had changed Florida law, thereby sacrificing the opportunity for the state to take advantage of the safe harbor. There were three central aspects to Bush's brief on this issue. First, it pointed to Florida statutes that set November 14 as a date for counties to submit vote totals and argued that the Florida Supreme Court's extension of that date to November 26 constituted a rewriting of Florida law. Second, the Bush brief pointed to the Florida Supreme Court's ruling that the secretary of state could reject manual recount tallies only to (a) ensure a losing candidate time to contest the election or (b) ensure compliance with federal electoral deadlines. That ruling, too, said Bush, was an act of judicial legislation. Third, Bush pointed to the Florida high court's various invocations of its "equitable powers," signals, claimed Bush, that the state court was legislating, rather than interpreting.

Bush next charged that the Florida Supreme Court had rewritten state law and thereby violated Article II of the U.S. Constitution. Article II grants to state legislatures the power to determine the manner of choosing electors. Bush's contention was that the Florida high court had legislated, rather than interpreted, taking power away from the state legislature. Bush's brief discussed in detail the framers' decision to give power to state legislatures and explained that, although state legislatures could authorize state courts to play a role in the selection of electors, the authorization must be explicit. In Florida, argued Bush, the laws delegate to the people the power to pick the electors and delegate to the secretary of state and other officials various powers regarding vote counting and certification. The state high court, said Bush, overstepped its bounds by extending the vote counting until November 26 and in so doing violated the federal constitutional principle that only the state legislatures may determine the manner for choosing electors.

Gore's primary response to both Bush arguments was that the Florida Supreme Court had simply interpreted conflicting provisions of Florida law, in light of the Florida Constitution's commitment to the right to vote. The state's high court, said Gore, had always relied on various rules of statutory construction to resolve messy statutory problems, and it had done no different here. Furthermore, the Florida legislature had established a system for judicial review of various issues, including issues arising during elections. The state supreme court was relying on these legislatively granted powers.

Gore added an argument about the safe-harbor provision. It is, he pointed out, an "option, not a mandate."[2] In other words, the safe-harbor provision does not prevent a state from relying on postelection day law in resolving judicial contests. Rather, it provides an incentive to conclude such contests no later than December 12 and according to law in existence on election day. But an incentive is not a prohibition, so, even if one assumes, merely for purposes of argument, that the state court crafted postelection day law, that would eliminate Florida's opportunity to take advantage of the safe harbor, but it would violate no legal rule. A separate Gore argument suggested that if the safe-harbor provision is in fact a command to the states, such a command might violate the federal constitutional power of state legislatures to determine the manner for choosing electors. That is, Gore took one of Bush's main arguments and turned it back on Bush. If state legislatures have the federal constitutional power to determine the manner for selecting electors, then how can Congress, through the safe-harbor provision, insist that states wrap up judicial proceedings by a specific date and according to a limited set of rules? Congress, after all, has to follow the Constitution too.

So the parties filed their briefs, made their oral arguments,[3] and waited for the Court to rule. It did so three days after arguments, on Monday, December 4, and it issued a unanimous, unsigned opinion. Given the highly contentious and deeply political nature of the case, and given that the Court is itself generally divided between five so-called conservative Justices and four so-called liberal Justices, a unanimous opinion could mean only one thing—that the Court had basically decided not to decide. The Court had various ways of doing this. It could have dismissed the appeal entirely. It could have decided that the case was not ripe—that is, that the petitioner, here Bush, did not yet face harm that needed remedying. It could have decided that the case was moot—that is, that any harm Bush might have faced was no longer present. It could have decided that the case presented a "political question"—in other words, it could have held that the legal issues, however important, are best resolved by branches of the government other than the U.S. Supreme Court. All of these techniques of avoiding hard questions were available to the Court in this case, but it picked another option.

It sent the case back to the state high court for clarification. Here is how the Court got to this rather anticlimactic conclusion. It began by stating: "As a general rule, this Court defers to a state court's interpretation of a state statute."[4] The Court added, however, that, in the setting of a presidential election, Article II of the federal Constitution grants to state legislatures the power to determine the manner of choosing electors. Perhaps, therefore, the normal deference accorded state court interpretations of state law might have to yield. The Court did not, though, offer an opinion on whether the Florida Supreme Court had legislated, rather than interpreted, which was, of course, the core of Bush's appeal.

The Court's concern was with a different aspect of the state court's opinion. It was troubled by the possibility that the Florida Supreme Court had relied on the state constitution when interpreting Florida election law. As explained in chapter 7, a minor Bush argument became a major one during oral argument when Justice Scalia raised this concern about state constitutions. The *McPherson* case seemed to say that, in the unique setting of presidential elections, state constitutions may not play their usual role of limiting state legislative power, for that would violate the federal Article II grant to state legislatures of the power to determine the "manner" of choosing electors. After quoting the key language from *McPherson,* the Court in responding to Bush's appeal said this:

There are expressions in the opinion of the Supreme Court of Florida that may be read to indicate that it construed the Florida Election Code without regard to the extent to which the Florida Constitution could, consistent with [Article II], "circumscribe the legislative power."[5]

The Court then quoted a few passages from the Florida high court's opinion that referred to the right to vote conferred by the state constitution. The Court did not issue a ruling on the substance of the matter. It did not, that is, decide whether a state court may rely on a state constitution in a presidential election case or what the contours of such reliance may be. Remember that the key language in *McPherson* suggesting that state statutes trump state constitutions, in the presidential election setting, was "dicta," meaning language not necessary for decision of the case. The Court in Bush's appeal was, accordingly, free (in the sense of not being bound by precedent) to hold whatever it wanted on this question of the role of state constitutions. But, although it had such freedom, it failed to exercise it. Instead, it said this: "[W]e are unclear as to the extent to which the Florida Supreme Court saw the Florida Constitution as circumscribing the legislature's authority under [Article II]."[6]

The Court also said that the Florida high court had cited but not discussed the federal law provisions covering the electoral vote. The Court added:

Since § 5 [the safe-harbor section] contains a principle of federal law that would assure finality of the State's determination if made pursuant to a state law in effect before the election, a legislative wish to take advantage of the "safe harbor" would

counsel against any construction of the Election Code that
Congress might deem to be a change in the law.[7]

The Court did not hold that the Florida Supreme Court had, in
construing the election code, changed the law, and it did not
hold that the Florida legislature had expressed a wish to take advantage of the safe harbor provided by federal law. It simply
raised these matters as a concern and concluded, "We are . . . unclear as to the consideration the Florida Supreme Court accorded to [the safe-harbor provision]."[8]

So the U.S. Supreme Court was unclear about two aspects of
the Florida Supreme Court's ruling. Accordingly, relying on a
1940 opinion in which it had sent a case back to the Minnesota
Supreme Court because there was "considerable uncertainty as
to the precise grounds for the [state court's] decision,"[9] the
Court sent the case back to the Florida Supreme Court "for further proceedings not inconsistent with this opinion."[10] That is
standard language when the nation's high court remands a case
to a lower court. In this case, the task for the Florida Supreme
Court was to clarify (a) the extent of its reliance on Florida's constitution and (b) whether and how it took account of the safe-harbor provision of federal law. Furthermore, the U.S. Supreme
Court had not just remanded the case to the state high court; it
also had vacated the judgment of that court. It did not, though
"reverse" the judgment of the state court. A reversal would have
required holding that the Florida Supreme Court got something
wrong. But an order "vacating" the state court's judgment was
nonetheless significant. That meant the state court ruling extending the deadline for manual recounting until November 26
was set aside. The Bush forces could have gone into state court
and argued that all manual recount tallies after November 14
should be tossed out. However, November 26 had come and
gone, and on that date Secretary of State Harris had certified
Bush as the winner. Furthermore, Gore had already filed his con-

test action, and the parties were awaiting Judge Sauls's ruling on that action and then the Florida Supreme Court appeal from Judge Sauls's ruling. The Bush team did not press the issue of re-certifying the election according to pre-November 26 numbers.

On remand, the Florida Supreme Court called for briefs and then sat on the case. Over a seven-day period between the U.S. Supreme Court's request for clarification and the Florida Supreme Court's response, the following occurred: Judge Sauls ruled against the Gore contest, Gore appealed that ruling and won in the Florida Supreme Court, and the U.S. Supreme Court stayed (i.e., blocked) the Gore contest victory and held oral arguments on the merits of the case. During those arguments, held on Monday morning, December 11, Justice O'Connor in particular expressed concern that the Florida Supreme Court had not yet responded to the request for clarification on the issues of reliance on the state constitution and concern for the safe harbor. On the evening of December 11, hours after the conclusion of those U.S. Supreme Court oral arguments, the Florida Supreme Court finally issued its revised opinion, responding to the request for clarification.

The state high court resolved the statutory conflicts as it had done before, by use of various rules of statutory construction. It again concluded that the secretary of state had discretion to accept manual recount tallies filed after November 14 and again concluded that the only good reasons to reject such tallies at the protest stage would be to protect a losing candidate's right to contest an election and to heed federal electoral college deadlines. So its basic holding was the same, and its primary reliance on standard tools of statutory interpretation was the same. It did two things differently, however, obviously in response to the U.S. Supreme Court's request for clarification. First, it dropped all references to the state constitution. The references in the prior opinion were part of the basis for the court's conclusion that the secretary of state had a narrow scope of discretion to ignore manual recount tallies. In the revised opinion, having dropped references to a state constitutional right to vote, the court concluded instead that it could "foresee no reason why the Department [of State] would refuse to accept amended returns if a county was proceeding in good faith with a manual recount under [the protest provision]."[11] It added: "[W]e have identified the right of Florida's citizens to vote and to have elections determined by the will of Florida's voters as important policy concerns of the Florida Legislature in enacting Florida's election code."[12] So any possible issue regarding the state court's reliance on the state constitution to trump the state legislature had vanished. It is possible, though, that had this issue again reached the U.S. Supreme Court, that Court might have seen the Florida Supreme Court's revision of its opinion as pretextual, that is, it might have construed the quoted "policy concerns of the Florida Legislature" as a stand-in for a reference to the state constitution. But the matter never again arose.

Second, the state high court responded to the concern about the safe-harbor provision. While in the prior opinion it had merely cited, in a footnote, an assortment of federal electoral college provisions, in its revised opinion it brought the safe-harbor section—3 U.S.C. § 5—into a prominent place in its reasoning. It stated that the secretary of state could reject manual recounts at the protest stage if allowing them to continue would "result in Florida voters not participating fully in the federal electoral process, as provided in 3 U.S.C. § 5."[13] This explicit reference to the safe-harbor provision played a pivotal role in the U.S. Supreme Court's order the following day, terminating manual recounts in Florida, and thus ending the 2000 presidential election. That order, and the controversy surrounding it, is the subject of the next chapter.

Part III. The End of the Road

9. The U.S. Supreme Court Ends the Election

The Unconstitutionality of Florida's Hand Counts and the Ultimate Significance of December 12

On Tuesday night, December 12, at 10:00 P.M., the United States Supreme Court ended the election. As the networks had prematurely proclaimed on election night, George W. Bush would become our forty-third president. The events of the five-day period from December 8 through December 12 had been furiously fast-paced and dramatic. On December 8 the Florida Supreme Court, by a 4-3 vote, ruled for Gore in his election contest, added votes to his total, and ordered all of the state's undervotes manually recounted. Bush asked the U.S. Supreme Court to enjoin, or "stay," that state-court ruling and asked the Court to take his appeal and overturn the ruling. On December 9, after the hand recount had begun, the U.S. Supreme Court responded, voting 5-4 to stop the manual recounts and to hear Bush's appeal. On December 10, the parties filed their briefs with the Court. On the morning of December 11, the lawyers argued the case before a packed courtroom in Washington. On December 12, the Court issued its landmark ruling.

It held that the Florida system for manually recounting ballots was unconstitutional, that it violated the equal protection clause of the Fourteenth Amendment. Somewhat surprisingly, the vote on that issue was 7-2, with Justices Souter and Breyer, normally left-of-center, joining the five more conservative Justices. Only

Justices Stevens and Ginsburg voted to uphold the Florida system. But the agreement of Justices Souter and Breyer with the conservatives collapsed over the issue of what to do next. Souter and Breyer wanted to send the case back to Florida to give the state courts a chance to put into place a proper system for hand counting and to allow the hand counting to resume. The five conservative Justices would have nothing of that; they voted to end the election immediately. This chapter first discusses the stay order issued on December 9. It then summarizes the arguments both sides made to the Court, explains how the Court ruled and what the different Justices said in their opinions, and analyzes the crucial final ruling making December 12 the day the election must end.

On December 8, the Florida Supreme Court narrowly reversed Judge Sauls's ruling that threw out Gore's election contest. The state high court construed state election law as requiring votes identified for Gore but not added to his column to be added, and further interpreted state law to require hand counting of the undervotes, not only in the counties Gore requested but also statewide, to avoid a constitutional problem of selectivity. But the next day the U.S. Supreme Court, in a brief order, granted Bush's application to stay the effect of that state-court ruling. Justice Stevens dissented, joined by Justices Souter, Ginsburg, and Breyer. Stevens wrote that the majority had "depart[ed] from three venerable rules of judicial restraint that have guided the Court throughout its history."[1] First, the Court usually respects what state courts say on questions of state law. Here, most of Bush's case involved disagreement with the Florida high court's interpretation of Florida law. Second, the Court usually construes its jurisdiction narrowly when other branches of federal government have power to resolve disputes. Here, the federal electoral college statutes give Congress authority to sort out problems with electoral votes. Third, some of the federal constitutional questions in the case had not been fairly presented to the Florida Supreme Court. This would usually be a good reason for the U.S. Supreme Court to keep away from the case.

Stevens then turned to the issue of irreparable harm. To obtain a stay order, which means that the Court prevents a lower court's order from having any effect, a party must show that it is not enough for the Court eventually to rule in its favor and award a remedy. Instead, the party must show that any remedy awarded at a later date would be insufficient to correct the harm. An easy example of a claim of irreparable injury is that of a death-row inmate who asks for a stay of execution so that the Court may hear his appeal. Obviously, if the Court hears the appeal but refuses to issue the stay order, any later ruling on the inmate's behalf would be fruitless. Justice Stevens thought that there was no harm to Bush from hand counting that could not be rectified later. Stevens wrote, "Counting every legally cast vote cannot constitute irreparable harm."[2] If votes were counted by hand and the Court decided after briefing and argument that the votes should not have been counted, then the Court could exclude those votes. Stevens added that issuing a stay might, in fact, irreparably harm Gore, rather than Bush. Finally, Stevens added some thoughts about the merits of the case, suggesting that the Florida system violated neither federal law nor the federal Constitution.

Justice Scalia, who had voted with the majority, wrote a brief concurring opinion responding to Justice Stevens's dissent. Scalia offered two reasons to support Bush's claim of irreparable harm. First, Scalia wrote:

The counting of votes that are of questionable legality does in my view threaten irreparable harm to petitioner [Bush], and to the country, by casting a cloud upon what he claims to be the legitimacy of his election. Count first, and rule upon legality afterwards, is not a recipe for producing election results that have the public acceptance democratic stability requires.[3]

Second, Scalia maintained that if the counting went forward and was later ruled unlawful, then it would be difficult to get an accurate recount afterward, "since it is generally agreed that each manual recount produces a degradation of the ballots."[4]

The theory that Bush would be irreparably harmed by a vote count that went in Gore's favor but then had to be reversed because of legal error is unusual, to say the least. The principal harm to Bush—that votes counted for Gore should not have been—would be remedied by a subsequent Court order excluding such votes. So the Court was left with the main theory articulated by Justice Scalia, namely that a cloud would be cast on the legitimacy of Bush's election should a Florida win for Gore be reversed because of a legal ruling from the U.S. Supreme Court. Even assuming that this turn of events would harm Bush, it is hard to see how it would *irreparably* harm Bush. The repair of this harm would come with time, with Bush's taking the helm and the public's gradual acceptance of him as president.

The parties filed their briefs on the merits the next day. The first two questions Bush presented were replicas of the questions the Court had examined in the first Bush appeal. He again argued that the Florida Supreme Court had legislated, rather than interpreted, thereby usurping the powers of the Florida Legislature. In the prior case, his concern was with the state court's construction of protest-stage law, allowing counties to continue hand counting until November 26. In this case, Bush's argument was with the state court's interpretation of contest-stage law. The Florida high court had read the phrase "rejection of legal votes" literally and expansively. The state court had added votes to Gore's totals that officials had rejected and had insisted on a statewide manual recount of undervotes, which machines had rejected. This reading of state law, and the remedial scheme ordered, was so unreasonable, Bush argued, that it must be seen as legislation, rather than interpretation. Accordingly, said Bush, both federal law and the federal Constitution were violated, in precisely the same ways as he had suggested in the earlier case. Thus, Bush argued that the state court had deprived Florida of the chance to protect its electors from challenge, for the safe-harbor provision kicks in only if the state courts make no changes to the law when deciding election contests. Also, Bush argued that the state court had violated Article II of the federal Constitution, which gives state legislatures, not state courts, the power to determine the manner of choosing electors.

Gore's response to these arguments was similar to his response at the protest stage. The Florida Supreme Court, said Gore, had interpreted Florida statutes. It did not rewrite law; it did not legislate. Although one might disagree with the Florida high court's reading of Florida law, that is a dispute over the meaning of state law, and federal courts have no role to play in resolving state-law disputes. Accordingly, neither Article II of the U.S. Constitution nor the safe-harbor provision of federal law had been violated.

The third question presented by Bush was whether the Florida system for manual recounts violates the Fourteenth Amendment of the U.S. Constitution, specifically the equal protection clause and the due process clause. Bush had raised this issue before, in his first appeal, but the Court had excluded it from consideration at that time. Now, though, the Court was ready to hear this challenge. Bush argued that neither state law nor the state high court had specified what "voter's intent" means, thus leaving ballot determinations to the "unbridled discretion and arbitrary decisionmaking of local election officials"[5] and others who might be involved in the vote counting. Without guidance from law, argued Bush, "there is a very substantial risk that the method for determining how to count a vote will be influenced, consciously or unconsciously, by individual desire for a particular result."[6] Moreover, different counties had used and were using different standards for manual recounts.

In response to these arguments, Gore pointed out that Florida law implements procedures to ensure fairness in vote counting. Specifically, he noted that Florida law permits the public and representatives of the political parties to observe hand recounts and that courts review disputed ballots to ensure consistency in applying the voter-intent standard. Additionally, Gore argued that many legal standards are somewhat broad and subject to varying application. As an example, he cited the obvious problems in interpreting "negligence" in various factual settings. But, just as there will be some degree of variance in applying a standard such as negligence, so, too, will there be some degree of variance in applying a standard such as voter's intent. Adoption of Bush's argument that the Constitution requires more precise standards to be applied in all Florida counties would mean that every state must reexamine its election laws to ensure that counties look at votes in a specific and uniform fashion. The Supreme Court has never suggested that this is a constitutional requirement, said Gore.

After receiving the briefs and hearing oral arguments,[7] the Supreme Court ruled that the Florida system for manual recounts violates the equal protection clause of the Fourteenth Amendment and also ruled that there was no time for the state to resume hand counting under a revised, constitutional scheme. The principal opinion was signed by no particular Justice but rather was issued as "per curiam," or "for the Court." It was almost certainly written by either Justice O'Connor, Justice Kennedy, or both, because they are the only Justices who didn't join one of the concurring or dissenting opinions. By examining those separate opinions, it is clear that only five Justices joined the principal opinion for the Court: Chief Justice Rehnquist and Justices O'Connor, Scalia, Kennedy, and Thomas. In addition to joining the majority opinion, Chief Justice Rehnquist wrote a separate concurring opinion, joined by Justices Scalia and Thomas. They agreed that the Florida system violated equal protection, but they also concluded that the Florida high court had changed the law, thereby violating Article II of the Constitution and the safe-harbor provision of federal law. Justice Stevens, Justice Souter, Justice Ginsburg, and Justice Breyer each wrote a dissent, and each dissent was joined to varying degrees by the other dissenters. Justices Souter and Breyer, although dissenting from the disposition of the case halting further manual recounts, were in substantial agreement with the majority's conclusion that the Florida system violated the equal protection clause. In sum, the fairest way to characterize the vote is 7-2 to hold unconstitutional the Florida system for manual recounts, but only 5-4 to stop the recounting, rather than remand to Florida for further counting under a revised, and constitutional, system.

After reciting the facts, the Court resolved the case in a fairly brief opinion. The Court began by offering a suggestion for state legislatures across the nation:

This case has shown that punch card balloting machines can produce an unfortunate number of ballots which are not punched in a clean, complete way by the voter. After the current counting, it is likely legislative bodies nationwide will examine ways to improve the mechanisms and machinery for voting.[8]

State legislatures, the Court continued, have uniformly granted to citizens the power to choose presidential electors. Once granted, that right to vote is fundamental; the Constitution demands the "equal weight accorded to each vote and the equal dignity owed to each voter."[9] Both sides agree on this general proposition, said the Court. The question is "whether the recount procedures the Florida Supreme Court has adopted are consistent with its obligation to avoid arbitrary and disparate treatment of the members of its electorate."[10] The state high court had ordered manual recounts under Florida law, requiring officials to determine voter intent. The Court continued:

> This is unobjectionable as an abstract proposition and a starting principle. The problem inheres in the absence of specific standards to ensure its equal application. The formulation of uniform rules to determine intent based on these recurring circumstances is practicable and, we conclude, necessary.[11]

The Court acknowledged that law often requires evidence of intent, and sometimes an "intent" standard cannot be further refined. The question here, though, is

> not whether to believe a witness but how to interpret the marks or holes or scratches on an inanimate object, a piece of cardboard or paper which, it is said, might not have registered as a vote during the machine count. The factfinder confronts a thing, not a person. The search for intent can be confined by specific rules designed to ensure uniform treatment.[12]

Unfortunately, the lack of such rules in Florida had led to non-uniformity: "[T]he standards for accepting or rejecting contested ballots might vary not only from county to county but indeed within a single county from one recount team to another."[13] In ruling for Gore in the election contest, the state supreme court had furthered the uneven treatment that the state statute enables. The court had included vote totals from different counties that had used different standards for determining voter intent.

Addressing the details of the state court's order for a manual recount of all the undervotes, the Court expressed concern that overvotes (i.e., double-punched ballots) would not be recounted. The Court was also concerned that in at least one county (Miami-Dade), the state court had ordered inclusion of a partial recount. Moreover, the state court had not specified who would recount the statewide undervotes. The Court found all of this troublesome:

> [W]e are presented with a situation where a state court with the power to assure uniformity has ordered a statewide recount with minimal procedural safeguards. When a court orders a statewide remedy, there must be at least some assurance that the rudimentary requirements of equal treatment and fundamental fairness are satisfied.[14]

A manual recount in Florida could not, said the Court, be completed constitutionally "without substantial additional work"[15]:

> It would require not only the adoption (after opportunity for argument) of adequate statewide standards for determining what is a legal vote, and practicable procedures to implement them, but also orderly judicial review of any disputed matters that might arise. In addition, the Secretary of State has advised that the recount of only a portion of the ballots requires that the vote tabulation equipment be used to screen out undervotes, a function for which the machines were not designed. If a recount of overvotes were also required, perhaps even a second screening would be necessary. Use of the equipment for this purpose, and any new software developed for it, would have to be evaluated for accuracy by the Secretary of State. . . .[16]

Seven Justices agreed that "there are constitutional problems with the recount ordered by the Florida Supreme Court that demand a remedy."[17] There was disagreement, however, over what sort of order to issue, and the choice was stark. The Court could send the case back to Florida for implementation of constitutional standards and allow a resumed recount,[18] or it could stop the election in its tracks and permit no further counting. The majority, by a 5-4 vote, chose the latter.

The decision turned on the relevance of the safe-harbor provision of federal law and on the December 12 deadline for that safe harbor. As discussed earlier, the safe-harbor provision is conditional. It doesn't require a state to complete a judicial contest no later than December 12. Rather, it offers the incentive of a safe harbor, a protection from further challenge over electoral slates, if that deadline is met. States can choose whether or not to meet the deadline. The question was whether Florida had expressed such a desire. If it had, then the election had to end, for it was already 10:00 P.M. on December 12 when the U.S. Supreme Court ruled. Any further hand counting would take the state past December 12 and would eliminate the safe-harbor option. If, however, the state had not expressed a desire to choose the safe-harbor option, then the case could be sent back to the Florida Supreme Court, to give that court a crack at implementing a clearer, uniform, constitutional counting system. Such counting could continue until at least December 18, the date for electors to cast their votes for president across the nation, and perhaps until early January, when Congress was to meet to count those votes.

The majority opinion held that Florida had opted for the protection of the safe harbor. The Court wrote:

The Supreme Court of Florida has said that the legislature intended the State's electors to "participat[e] fully in the federal electoral process," as provided in 3 U.S.C. § 5 [the safe-harbor provision]. __ So.2d at __ (slip op. at 27); see also *Palm Beach Canvassing Bd. v. Harris*, 2000 WL 1725434, *13 (Fla. 2000). That statute, in turn, requires that any controversy or contest that is designed to lead to a conclusive selection of electors be completed by December 12. That date is upon us, and there is no recount procedure in place under the State Supreme Court's order that comports with minimal constitutional standards. Because it is evident that any recount seeking to meet the December 12 date will be unconstitutional for the reasons we have discussed, we reverse the judgment of the Supreme Court of Florida ordering a recount to proceed.[19]

Thus, the Supreme Court of the United States ended the presidential election. George W. Bush had won Florida, 2,912,790 to 2,912,253, and had won the presidency.

But did the counting have to stop on December 12? The Court did not exercise its own judgment in holding that December 12 was the last day for counting votes. Rather, the Court deferred to what the state supreme court had said. If the U.S. Supreme Court correctly construed the opinion of the Florida Supreme Court, then its conclusion that the counting must end immediately was sound. The state supreme court has the power to interpret Florida law as opting for the protection of the safe harbor, and it is the responsibility of the U.S. Supreme Court to defer to the state's wishes regarding the safe harbor. But if the U.S. Supreme Court misunderstood the Florida Supreme Court's opinion, then it ended the counting too soon. What exactly did the Florida Supreme Court say on the issue of the safe harbor?

According to the U.S. Supreme Court, as quoted above, "The Supreme Court of Florida has said that the legislature intended the State's electors to 'participat[e] fully in the federal electoral process,' as provided in 3 U.S.C. § 5 [the safe-harbor provision]."

Unfortunately, this statement is incorrect. The Florida Supreme Court opinion referred to is the revised opinion from the protest-stage case, which the state high court issued in response to the U.S. Supreme Court's request for clarification. The U.S. Supreme Court was concerned about whether the state court had taken the safe-harbor provision into account when it issued its protest-stage ruling. In response, the Florida Supreme Court said that manual recounts must be included in vote tallies, before a winner is certified, unless this would jeopardize either the losing candidate's opportunity to contest the election or the state's ability to take advantage of the safe-harbor date of December 12. The Florida Supreme Court did not claim to be interpreting statutes passed by the state legislature. It could not have made such a claim, because there is nothing in Florida law that refers to a desire to take advantage of the safe-harbor date, or not to do so.[20] Florida law is silent on the subject. The Florida Supreme Court's clarification, therefore, was not a report on Florida law. Instead, it was a response to the U.S. Supreme Court's concern that the state court had not itself adequately thought about the safe-harbor date when extending the deadline for manual recounts at the protest stage. To the extent that the U.S. high court ordered the counting stopped on December 12 because it thought that's what Florida statutes require, that conclusion was simply wrong. Moreover, had the Florida legislature addressed the issue as a general policy matter, it might well have chosen to ensure that all ballots are accurately counted, rather than adhere to a nonmandatory federal timetable.

There is more to be said, though, regarding whether Florida had in fact opted for the protection of the safe harbor, thus making December 12 the appropriate date for the election to end. The U.S. Supreme Court—perhaps because of the speed with which the Justices wrote the opinions—simply goofed in stating that the Florida Supreme Court had said anything about what the Florida legislature intended regarding the safe harbor. As mentioned, Florida statutes are silent on the subject. But the Florida Supreme Court, in its revised protest-stage opinion, had lots to say about the safe harbor, including some important statements that the U.S. Supreme Court overlooked.

In addition to the state high court's concern that Florida voters "participat[e] fully in the federal electoral process, as provided in 3 U.S.C. § 5" (which the court said twice), consider these two footnotes from the state court's opinion:

> What is a reasonable time required for completion [of a manual recount at the protest stage] will, in part, depend on whether the election is for a statewide office, for a federal office or for presidential electors. In the case of the presidential election, the determination of reasonableness must be circumscribed by the provisions of 3 U.S.C. § 5, which sets December 12, 2000 as the date for final determination of any state's dispute concerning its electors in order for that determination to be given conclusive effect in Congress.[21]

> [I]t is necessary to read all provisions of the elections code in pari materia [i.e., together, as a whole]. In this case, that comprehensive reading required that there be time for an elections contest pursuant to section 102.168, which all parties had agreed was a necessary component of the statutory scheme and to accommodate the outside deadline set forth in 3 U.S.C. § 5 of December 12, 2000.[22]

Taking all these statements together, it is reasonable to suggest that the Florida Supreme Court thought that all manual recounts must end no later than December 12. One might respond, though, that these statements were made in the context of setting time limits for manual recounts during an election protest, when county canvassing boards are still counting ballots. The statements were not made in the context of an election contest, when the losing candidate challenges the winner's certification. Perhaps the state court, in a contest case, would not view December 12 as the drop-dead date for counting ballots.

There is some evidence, though, that the state court viewed December 12 as the end of all counting, protest or contest. Consider these two footnotes from its opinion upholding Gore's contest challenge, issued Friday, December 8:

> The dissents would have us throw up our hands and say that because of looming deadlines and practical difficulties we should give up any attempt to have the election of the presidential electors rest upon the vote of Florida citizens as mandated by the Legislature. While we agree that practical difficulties may well end up controlling the outcome of the election we vigorously disagree that we should therefore abandon our responsibility to resolve this election dispute under the rule of law.[23]

> We are mindful of the fact that due to time constraints, the count of the undervotes places demands on the public servants throughout the State to work over this week-end. However, we are confident that with the cooperation of the officials in all the counties, the [count of the] remaining undervotes in these counties can be accomplished within the required time frame.[24]

The strong implication of these statements, especially when combined with the ones quoted above from the protest-stage revised opinion, is that the Florida Supreme Court thought all manual recounts—whether protest or contest—must be completed no later than December 12.

Does this mean that the U.S. Supreme Court was correct in deeming Florida to have opted for the protection of the safe harbor? Not necessarily. It depends on what the Florida Supreme Court meant by its various references, explicit and implicit, to

December 12. The state high court could not have meant to refer to state statutes, because, as mentioned, Florida statutes say nothing about opting in or out of the safe-harbor protection. That leaves only two explanations. One is that the state court was choosing for Florida, saying what it believed the Florida legislature would say were it faced with the question (in the abstract, not limited to this election) whether to allow manual recounts past the safe-harbor date. A state court has the power to construe the landscape of state law, even if there is no express statute on the subject. The other explanation is that the state court understood the safe-harbor provision as mandatory rather than conditional, and thus that the state lacked the authority to count votes past December 12. This understanding would have been beyond the power of the Florida Supreme Court. For although state courts are supreme in interpreting state law, they must yield on interpretations of federal law. A state-court understanding that the safe-harbor provision is absolute rather than conditional would be a misreading of federal law, and could be set aside by a federal court in an appropriate case.

This lack of clarity about the Florida Supreme Court's views on the safe-harbor provision should have resulted in a remand to that court for clarification. That's what the U.S. Supreme Court did in the first, protest-stage case, and it's what it should have done (with even greater justification) in the second, contest-stage case. Granted, such a remand, and further proceedings in the state court, would have taken even more precious time. But, if upon reflection (and after briefing) the state court had realized and clearly stated that it understood the safe harbor to be an option, not a requirement, and if it had focused on whether a contest should be allowed to continue past the safe-harbor date, it might well have construed the landscape of Florida law as opting for votes to be counted.

☐

Besides the majority opinion, there was a concurrence and four dissents. Chief Justice Rehnquist wrote the concurring opinion, joined by Justices Scalia and Thomas. In addition to supporting the majority's equal protection holding and its order that the counting halt, Rehnquist accepted Bush's arguments that the state high court had rewritten Florida law, thereby violating both Article II of the federal Constitution and the safe-harbor provision of federal law. "Isolated sections of [Florida law] may well admit of more than one interpretation," said Rehnquist, "but the general coherence of the legislative scheme may not be altered by judicial interpretation so as to wholly change the statutorily provided apportionment of responsibility among [various state bodies and officials]."[25] Here are the ways in which Rehnquist concluded that the state supreme court had rewritten, rather than interpreted, Florida law:

(a)   Although state law grants discretion over recounts to county canvassing boards, the state court gave no deference to the decisions of those boards.

(b)   By insisting that votes be included past the certification deadline, the state court violated that deadline and improperly displaced the secretary of state's discretion to ignore late-filed tallies.

(c)   State law provides instructions to voters to check their ballots before submitting them and provides for countywide manual recounts if machines do not count ballots properly. The state court nonetheless determined that a vote is a legal one, and must be included in the tallies, even if a voter disregards the instructions and even if the machines work properly. "[T]here is no basis for reading the Florida statutes as requiring the counting of improperly marked ballots. . . ."[26]

Like the Bush attack on the Florida Supreme Court in the protest-stage case, this attack on the Florida Supreme Court was quite weak. The reason is not that the Florida Supreme Court's interpretation of "rejection of legal votes" is clearly correct. As discussed in chapter 4, the Bush reading of that key phrase was strong, perhaps even stronger than the reading the state high court ultimately adopted. But, for purposes of review by the U.S. Supreme Court—which is a federal court, without general jurisdiction to review questions of state law—the issue was whether the Florida Supreme Court's interpretation of "rejection of legal votes" was so unreasonable as to constitute a judicial rewriting of the statute. That clearly was not the case, for "rejection of legal votes" is a vague phrase that can reasonably be interpreted in various ways.

Each of the four dissenters filed an opinion. Justice Stevens began his dissent, which Justices Ginsburg and Breyer joined, by stating that the Court should never have become involved in what is primarily a matter of Florida law. The safe-harbor provision, Stevens added, imposes no "affirmative duties upon the States that their governmental branches could 'violate.'"[27] To the contrary, the provision is a conditional one, merely offering an incentive for states to wrap up contests no later than December 12. Even if there were a constitutional violation involving the system for manual recounts, the Court was wrong to stop the counting, rather than to give Florida an opportunity to correct its error and count anew. But, for Stevens, there was no underlying constitutional violation. "Intent of the voter" is a standard like many other legal standards. Stevens gave the example of "beyond a reasonable doubt," the burden of proof a prosecutor must satisfy in a criminal trial. The county canvassing boards can reach reasonably consistent applications of "voter's intent"; if not, then "a single impartial magistrate will ultimately adjudicate all objections arising from the recount process."[28] After differing with Chief Justice Rehnquist about whether the Florida Supreme Court legislated, rather than interpreted, Justice Stevens concluded with what will likely become one of his most memorable statements:

What must underlie petitioners' entire federal assault on the
Florida election procedures is an unstated lack of confidence
in the impartiality and capacity of the state judges who would
make the critical decisions if the vote count were to proceed.
Otherwise, their position is wholly without merit. The en-
dorsement of that position by the majority of this Court can
only lend credence to the most cynical appraisal of the work of
judges throughout the land. It is confidence in the men and
women who administer the judicial system that is the true back-
bone of the rule of law. Time will one day heal the wound to
that confidence that will be inflicted by today's decision. One
thing, however, is certain. Although we may never know with
complete certainty the identity of the winner of this year's Presidential election, the identity of the loser is perfectly clear. It is
the Nation's confidence in the judge as an impartial guardian
of the rule of law.[29]

The last two sentences have a double meaning. They appear to
be a critique of the majority of the United States Supreme Court.
But, understood in the context of the entire paragraph, they also
express concern about the majority's attack on the Florida Supreme Court.

Justice Souter also dissented, joined by Justice Breyer, and by
Justices Stevens and Ginsburg except as to Souter's conclusion
regarding the constitutionality of the Florida manual recount system. Souter began by criticizing the Court for taking both of
Bush's appeals and for staying the hand counting. As to the safe-
harbor issue, he agreed with Justice Stevens that, because the federal law is conditional rather than absolute, the state high court
could not violate it. As to the Article II argument that the state
high court had usurped the prerogatives of the state legislature,
Souter concluded, "None of the state court's interpretations is
unreasonable to the point of displacing" the legislature's pow-

ers.[30] First, state law does not define "legal vote," so the state court had to do so to resolve Gore's contest challenge. Its reading of "legal vote" to mean any ballot from which a clear indication of voter's intent could be discerned was a reasonable one. Second, it was reasonable for the state court to read "rejection" of legal votes as either a human or machine failure to count a vote. Third, the state court reasonably determined that a recount of undervotes was necessary because those votes might "place in doubt" the outcome of the election, as specified in Florida law.

On the equal protection issue, Justice Souter agreed with the majority opinion. Although states may generally choose varying voting methods and may allow counties to vary, this case presented a different problem:

> [E]vidence in the record here suggests that a different order of disparity obtains under rules for determining a voter's intent that have been applied (and could continue to be applied) to identical types of ballots used in identical brands of machines and exhibiting identical physical characteristics (such as "hanging" or "dimpled" chads). . . . I can conceive of no legitimate state interest served by these differing treatments of the expressions of voters' fundamental rights. The differences appear wholly arbitrary.[31]

However, Souter disagreed with the majority that the counting had to stop immediately. He would have allowed the Florida courts to establish uniform standards and to allow the counting to continue until at least December 18, the date electors meet across the nation to vote for President.

Justice Ginsburg also dissented, joined by Justice Stevens, and by Justices Souter and Breyer except as to her conclusion that there was no equal protection violation. She began by disagreeing with Chief Justice Rehnquist that the Florida

Supreme Court's interpretation of Florida law had passed the bounds of reason. The U.S. Supreme Court generally defers to state court interpretations of state law. There is no reason, even in the context of a presidential election, to depart from this important rule regarding the balance of federal and state power, reasoned Justice Ginsburg. Next, she agreed with Justice Stevens that the Florida system did not violate equal protection. She added that, even had she differed on that point, she would have still allowed the counting to continue under revised standards. The majority was wrong, she argued, to insist that December 12 was a deadline. Federal electoral college statutes specify December 18 as the date for the electors to meet, and Congress counts electoral votes early in January. There is time for more counting, said Justice Ginsburg. "[T]he Court's conclusion that a constitutionally adequate recount is impractical," she added, "is a prophecy the Court's own judgment will not allow to be tested. Such an untested prophecy should not decide the Presidency of the United States."[32]

Finally, Justice Breyer dissented, joined by Justices Stevens and Ginsburg except as to his conclusion about the equal protection violation, and joined by Justice Souter except as to his discussion of the respective roles of the Court and the Congress in resolving presidential election disputes. He began by agreeing with the majority and Justice Souter that Florida's failure to provide "uniform subsidiary standards" for interpreting the intent of the voter violated the equal protection clause of the Fourteenth Amendment. But, disagreeing with the majority, he would have given the state courts a chance to put proper standards in place and to count until at least December 18. He then disagreed with Chief Justice Rehnquist that the Florida Supreme Court had gone beyond the bounds of reason in construing Florida's election code. Finally, he argued that both the Constitution, in the Twelfth Amendment, and Congress, by enacting laws giving itself the power to resolve electoral vote disputes, envision little or no role for the Court in such cases. He wrote: "Given this detailed, comprehensive scheme for counting electoral votes, there is no reason to believe that federal law either foresees or requires resolution of such a political issue by this Court."[33] The one time in history that members of the Court became actively involved in resolving a presidential election was the Hayes-Tilden debacle of 1876, and surely that lesson should have taught the Court to keep its hands off, said Justice Breyer. He added:

> [I]n this highly politicized matter, the appearance of a split decision runs the risk of undermining the public's confidence in the Court itself. That confidence is a public treasure. . . . [W]e do risk a self-inflicted wound—a wound that may harm not just the Court, but the Nation.[34]

And so it ended. By a 5-4 vote, the U.S. Supreme Court stopped the manual recount in Florida. The next day, Vice President Gore conceded the election, and Governor Bush made his first speech as president-elect. Was the Court correct, though, to view the Florida system for manual recounts as unconstitutional? Whatever one thinks about the Court's insistence on December 12 as a deadline, the Court was right to be troubled by the vagueness of the "voter's intent" standard and the inconsistent application of that standard among the counties. The Court pointed to two prior voting rights cases in which it had invalidated state election schemes because of differential treatment of voters based on county residence. In one, the state "accorded arbitrary and disparate treatment to voters in its different counties."[35] The state was using a system in which a citizen's vote counted for less as the size of the citizen's county of residence increased. In the other case, the "county-based procedure . . . diluted the influence of citizens in larger counties in the nominating process."[36]

Although these cases were helpful to the Court in assessing the Florida system for manual recounts, they were only obliquely on point because (a) the Florida system does not expressly value votes differently based on county of residence, and (b) the primary problem with the Florida system was the differential application of a vague standard.

There is a line of cases the Court did not cite that could have helped it reach the conclusion that the Florida system for conducting manual recounts was unconstitutional. In many freedom-of-speech and freedom-of-the-press cases, the Court has insisted that, when law gives discretion to public officials, that discretion must be bounded by clear, objective criteria.[37] For example, if city law gives a city official power to grant or deny parade permits, or power to grant or deny requests to use loudspeakers at a city hall gathering, that law will be upheld only if it sets forth detailed, neutral, objective standards for granting or denying the requests. Otherwise, if the law says, essentially, "grant or deny as best serves the public interest," then the official has an enormous opportunity, consciously or unconsciously, to help speakers whose views she favors and to harm speakers whose views she disfavors. Although the Court has never applied this line of cases in the voting rights setting, voting rights share with speech and press rights a core political nature—they are all part of our essential citizenship; they are what allow us, rather than officials, to remain in control of government. The concern in Florida that different officials would count votes in different ways based on the vague "voter's intent" standard was a concern with roots in these free-speech and free-press cases.

This understanding would allow the Court's key holding in *Bush v. Gore* to have a powerful but limited scope of application in future cases. Many have suggested that if *Bush v. Gore* stands for the proposition that votes in a particular contest on a ballot must all be cast or counted in the same way, much of election law nationwide would be unconstitutional, because votes are cast and counted in a multitude of ways across the country and across counties within states. Different voting devices and their counting mechanisms have different rates of error. There might, indeed, be sound reasons of public policy to insist on uniform methods for casting and counting votes for any particular contested election. But the holding of *Bush v. Gore* need not be thought to extend to this problem. If one moves away from the stated equal protection basis for the outcome, and instead adopts the First Amendment analysis offered here, then only a certain type of differentiation among voting and vote-counting methods would have to be invalidated. Courts should step in, under the First Amendment theory, only when a jurisdiction gives to officials relatively unconstrained discretion to determine what counts as a vote. For only in that setting do we need to police the conscious or unconscious bias of government officials.

Ten days after the U.S. Supreme Court ruled, the Florida Supreme Court issued a brief per curiam opinion on remand from the nation's high court. It recognized, as it had to, that the U.S. Supreme Court had held that manual recounts could not continue past December 12 and that December 12 had passed. Thus, it concluded that Gore could not prevail in his contest action. It suggested that the state legislature was the appropriate body to develop "a specific, uniform standard necessary to ensure equal application and to secure the fundamental right to vote throughout the State of Florida."[38] The judgment was unanimous, but Chief Justice Wells and Justice Harding concurred in the result only, refusing to join the suggestion to the state legislature. Justice Shaw wrote a concurrence that expounded on the right to vote, as well as on the need for "fairness, reliability, and predictability."[39] He also criticized the U.S. Supreme Court for improperly deciding the counting could not continue past December 12. That date was not a mandatory date, said Justice Shaw, and the Florida Supreme Court's reference to it was in the context of a protest-stage decision, not a contest-stage decision. For the U.S. Supreme Court to rely on the state court's references to December 12 was to "confuse apples and oranges."[40] However, added Justice Shaw, there was probably nothing the state court could have done to satisfy the U.S. Supreme Court's concerns.

Justice Pariente also wrote a concurrence. She offered recommendations for legislative action. First, she suggested that the legislature consider authorizing a candidate to ask for a statewide manual recount, rather than just county by county. If that change is not made, then at least county canvassing boards should rule on manual recount requests according to more specific standards, especially in statewide elections. Justice Pariente added that the legislature should consider more specific standards to ensure a uniform statewide assessment of voter's intent. Turning to the issue of counting undervotes, she obliquely criticized Secretary of State Harris for taking restrictive positions regarding vote counting. If the legislature were to adopt Harris's views, undervotes would often not be counted, and voters in counties that use punch-card systems would be disproportionately harmed, because the undervote rate is higher in such counties. Justice Pariente concluded by "applaud[ing] Governor Jeb Bush's creation of a Task Force that will study the state's elections process and recommend improvements to 'ensure the fairness of our system' and to fully modernize our voting and counting mechanisms."[41]

Part IV. The Wild-Card Lawsuits

10. The "Butterfly Ballot"

Palm Beach County and 3,407 Buchanan Votes

Though it had receded in importance by the time the Supreme Court ended the vote counting, the Palm Beach County
"butterfly ballot" was the center of attention immediately after
election day. Manual recounts had not yet captured center stage.
Although the butterfly ballot issue faded into the background, it
worked its way through the courts. Plaintiffs alleging that the ballot was illegal lost at the trial court level and again at the Florida
Supreme Court. The trial judge held that, even assuming the ballot was illegal, he had no authority to order a new election in the
county. The high court took the opposite approach, refusing to
rule on whether a revote could be ordered for a presidential election, dismissing the case instead on the ground that the butterfly
ballot was in substantial compliance with Florida law. But, even
though the butterfly ballot case ended without much fanfare, the
legal issues it presented were serious, and the underlying equitable argument never really went away. The claim of the dismayed Democratic voters—that thousands of them went to the
polling place to vote for Gore, but those votes never registered—
was always at the emotional core of Gore's argument that he had
really won Florida.

Figure 1 shows the butterfly ballot, which Palm Beach used for
the 2000 election. Candidates are displayed on both the left and

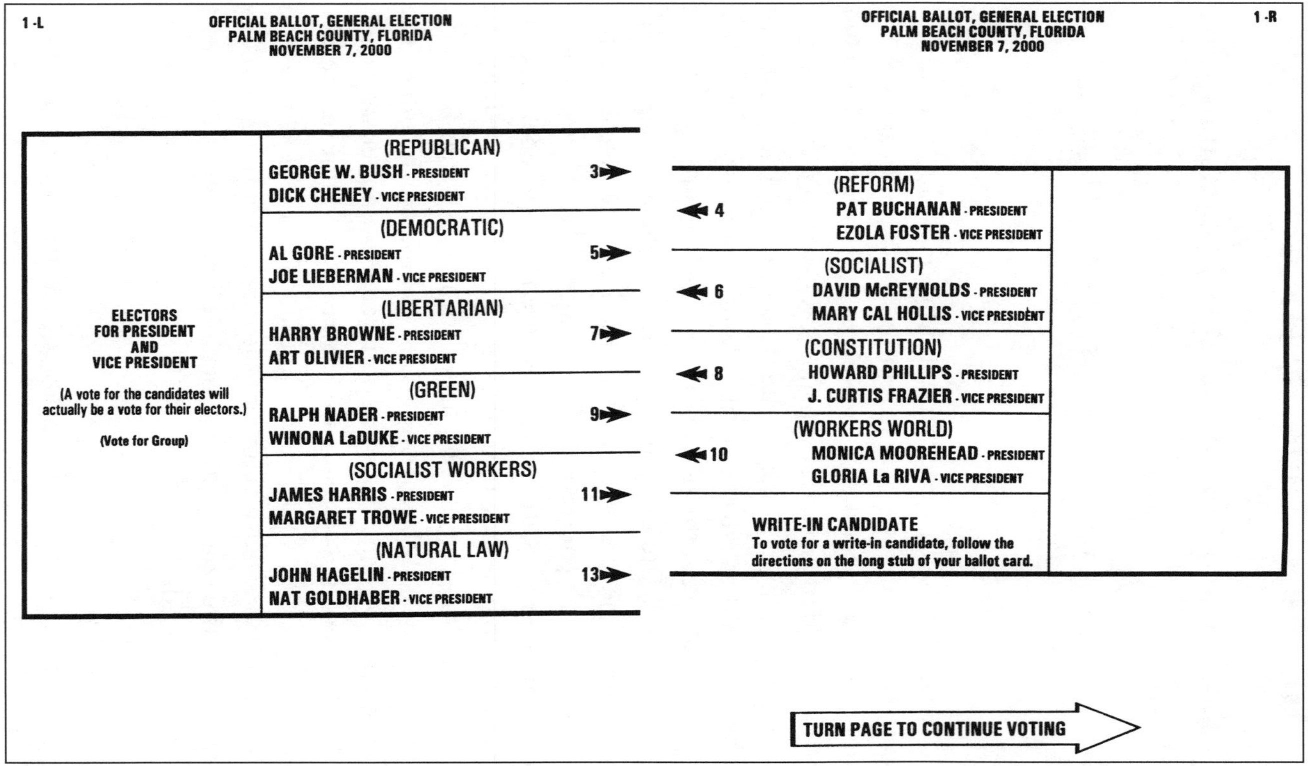
1 -L
OFFICIAL BALLOT, GENERAL ELECTION
PALM BEACH COUNTY, FLORIDA
NOVEMBER 7, 2000
ELECTORS FOR PRESIDENT AND VICE PRESIDENT
(A vote for the candidates will actually be a vote for their electors.)
(Vote for Group)
(REPUBLICAN)
GEORGE W. BUSH - PRESIDENT
DICK CHENEY - VICE PRESIDENT
3
(DEMOCRATIC)
AL GORE - PRESIDENT
JOE LIEBERMAN - VICE PRESIDENT
5
(LIBERTARIAN)
HARRY BROWNE - PRESIDENT
ART OLIVIER - VICE PRESIDENT
7
(GREEN)
RALPH NADER - PRESIDENT
WINONA LaDUKE - VICE PRESIDENT
9
(SOCIALIST WORKERS)
JAMES HARRIS - PRESIDENT
MARGARET TROWE - VICE PRESIDENT
11
(NATURAL LAW)
JOHN HAGELIN - PRESIDENT
NAT GOLDHABER - VICE PRESIDENT
13
OFFICIAL BALLOT, GENERAL ELECTION
PALM BEACH COUNTY, FLORIDA
NOVEMBER 7, 2000
1 -R
4
(REFORM)
PAT BUCHANAN - PRESIDENT
EZOLA FOSTER - VICE PRESIDENT
6
(SOCIALIST)
DAVID McREYNOLDS - PRESIDENT
MARY CAL HOLLIS - VICE PRESIDENT
8
(CONSTITUTION)
HOWARD PHILLIPS - PRESIDENT
J. CURTIS FRAZIER - VICE PRESIDENT
10
(WORKERS WORLD)
MONICA MOOREHEAD - PRESIDENT
GLORIA La RIVA - VICE PRESIDENT
WRITE-IN CANDIDATE
To vote for a write-in candidate, follow the directions on the long stub of your ballot card.
TURN PAGE TO CONTINUE VOTING

Figure 1.

the right (thus the two halves of the ballot page are like butterfly wings). A candidate's punch-hole is sometimes to the right of the candidate's name, sometimes to the left. The punch-holes are lined up in such a way that, although they are placed in the middle of a particular candidate's row, they also sit next to another candidate's row, on the other side of the ballot. In particular, note that Pat Buchanan's punch-hole is higher than Al Gore's punch-hole. Note also that the numbering of the punch-holes is Bush (3), Buchanan (4), then Gore (5). A voter expecting the Democrats, the second major party in the state, to have the second punch-hole on the ballot might well have punched that second hole, especially because it is lined up next to the black line over the Gore/Lieberman names.

When election results came in, Buchanan, the right-wing minor party candidate who would be the last person chosen by the elderly Jewish community that makes up a large portion of the Palm Beach vote, had gained 3,407 votes in the county. That was almost 2,400 more Buchanan votes than in any other county in Florida, and Palm Beach is a heavily Democratic county. It was 20 percent of Buchanan's statewide total. Gore outpolled Buchanan 167 to 1 across the state; in Palm Beach, that number was 79 to 1. In other Florida counties, Buchanan did best in precincts where Bush won a majority of the vote, which is to be expected, because those are generally more conservative precincts. In Palm Beach, Buchanan made his strongest showing in precincts where Gore had his strongest showing, adding to the argument that Gore voters mistakenly voted for Buchanan. In Bush's best Palm Beach precincts, Buchanan did more poorly than he did in Gore's best precincts. One statistical analysis showed that Buchanan would have won only 1,000 votes in Palm Beach had that county followed statewide voting patterns. Another statistician concluded, "Based on the relationship that we see in the data, the chances that this would happen just purely by accident or by chance would be significantly less than 1 in 1 trillion."[1] From all of this, it is hard to avoid the conclusion that the confusing butterfly ballot caused at least a few thousand Palm Beach voters who wanted to vote for Gore to vote instead for Buchanan by mistake. The number is certainly higher than 537, which is the margin by which Bush eventually won Florida.

In addition to the highly unusual Buchanan vote, there were 19,120 "double-punched" ballots in Palm Beach, that is, ballots on which a voter punched holes for two presidential candidates (also called the "overvote"). Such ballots are invalid under Florida law.[2] The overvote percentage in Palm Beach was high: 4.1 percent of all Palm Beach ballots were overvotes for the presidential race, compared with 2.7 percent in Miami-Dade County and 1.7 percent in Broward County. And the overvote in Palm Beach was more than six times the overvote in that county in the 1996 presidential election. It is fairly certain that Gore had a net loss of thousands of votes from the invalidated double-punched butterfly ballots.

The facts underneath the statistics tell the same story. Theresa LePore, the Palm Beach County elections supervisor and a Democrat, had designed the butterfly ballot so that elderly voters could read the presidential candidates' names in large print and see those names without having to flip pages. The ballot had been published in newspapers and mailed as a sample ballot, and no one had objected to it. One argument made later by many Palm Beach voters was that the punch-holes lined up more cleanly with candidates' names on the sample ballot than on the actual voting machines. On election day 2000 there was an enormous outcry from voters throughout the county. This helps show that the confusion was not a story made up after it was known that the election would come down to Florida. Many people were confused by the ballot. Some voters claimed that they mistakenly voted for Buchanan, realized the mistake, and asked for replacement ballot cards, as is permitted under Florida law, but were re-fused. Some voters asserted that they asked elections personnel on site for help, and in response some precinct workers followed instructions not to render assistance, so as to speed up voting. Some voters tried to get through to the swamped telephone lines at the county offices. Some voters called media outlets or Demo-cratic Party headquarters. Voters were calling their elected offi-cials; they were sharing stories, dismayed about the possibility of having voted for Buchanan by accident; some were in tears. By midafternoon, Supervisor LePore circulated a memo to pre-cincts advising poll workers to remind voters to be careful. But the 25 percent of Palm Beach voters who are elderly vote heavily in the early hours, so LePore's memo would not have helped them. And it is not clear how many precincts actually received the memo. As the Democrats learned about the problem, they frantically tried to get the message through to their voters to make sure they checked their ballots carefully, to make sure they had in fact voted for Gore. The Democrats also swiftly hired a firm to call their likely voters with the same message. During the ensuing week, thousands of Palm Beach voters swore out affidavits claiming they either had mistakenly voted for Bu-chanan when they intended to vote for Gore or had erroneously punched holes for two candidates.[3]

A few days after the election, voters in Palm Beach County who believed they might have mistakenly voted for Pat Buchanan sued to declare the butterfly ballot illegal. As a remedy, they demanded a new countywide vote for president. Both steps in the lawsuit—proving the ballot was illegal, and getting a judge to order a revote—were difficult, and neither eventually suc-ceeded. But the argument was fairly strong that the ballot was in fact illegal.

Punch-card ballots, such as those used in Palm Beach, are counted (at least initially) by machines. Thus, under Florida law, Palm Beach uses an "electronic or electromechanical voting system," which "means a system of casting votes by use of voting devices or marking devices and counting ballots by employing automatic tabulating equipment or data processing equipment."[4] This is relevant because it made the plaintiffs' argument somewhat more difficult. Had Palm Beach used paper ballots, where the voter marks his or her vote with an X and the ballots are counted by the human eye only, then three statutory provisions clearly would have applied, and each would just as clearly have been violated by the butterfly ballot. Here are the provisions:

(1) Beneath the caption and preceding the names of the candidates shall be the following words: "To vote for a candidate whose name is printed on the ballot, place a cross (X) mark in the blank space at the right of the name of the candidate for whom you desire to vote. . . ."[5]

(2) The names of the candidates of the party which received the highest number of votes for Governor in the last election in which a Governor was elected shall be placed first under the heading for each office . . . ; the names of the candidates of the party which received the second highest vote for Governor shall be second under the heading for each office. . . .[6]

(3) Minor political party candidates and candidates with no party affiliation shall have their names appear on the general election ballot following the names of recognized political parties. . . .[7]

The butterfly ballot did not conform to any of these rules.[8] First, some of punch-holes on the butterfly ballot were to the right of candidates' names (e.g., Bush and Gore), while other punch-holes were to the left of candidates' names (e.g., Buchanan). That violates rule (1), requiring voters to vote "at the right" of the candidate's name. Second, although the Democratic Party had finished second in the most recent gubernatorial election, arguably Gore's name did not appear second on the ballot. His punch-hole was below Buchanan's, and the Gore punch-hole number (5) came two after Bush's punch-hole number (3), with Buchanan's punch-hole number (4) coming in between. Furthermore, because Buchanan's name appeared higher on the ballot, arguably Gore's name was not second. All of this violates rule (2), granting the Democrats the second spot on the ballot. Third, although Buchanan was a minor political party candidate, arguably his name did not follow the Gore name, as required by rule (3), again because Buchanan's punch-hole was higher than Gore's, because his punch-hole number was higher in rank than Gore's, and because his name appeared higher on the ballot than Gore's. Thus, if the butterfly ballot were considered a paper ballot, it would be in violation of the state's election provisions.

But the butterfly ballot is counted by machine, and the rules stated above apply in "counties in which voting machines are not used."[9] However, the section of Florida election law that applied in Palm Beach—for counties that use "an electronic or electro-mechanical voting system"[10]—cross-references the paper ballot rules. It states: "The ballot information shall, as far as practicable, be in the order of arrangement provided for paper ballots."[11] There was nothing "impracticable" about making sure all punch-holes were to the right of a candidate's name in punch-card ballots, nor was there anything "impracticable" about making sure that Gore's name was clearly second and that Buchanan's name clearly followed Gore's. Thus, even though the butterfly ballot wasn't directly governed by the three rules listed, there was a strong argument that the rules applied by virtue of the cross-reference in the section that directly applied in Palm Beach.

Another section of the law that directly applied in Palm Beach was used against the Democratic plaintiffs, but the argument was not as strong as it seemed. The law provides that "Voting squares may be placed in front of or in back of the names of candidates. . . ."[12] Secretary of State Harris, among others, argued that the butterfly ballot was legal under this rule, because some voting squares (e.g., Buchanan's) came before the candidate's name, while other voting squares (e.g., Bush's and Gore's) came after the candidate's name. While this argument has some superficial appeal based on the text of the law, it is hard to believe the legislature expressly authorized ballots where, for the same race, some voting squares would be in front of and others in back of candidates' names. That is an obvious recipe for confusion. By far the more sensible reading of the rule is that on a given ballot, all voting squares must be either in front of candidates' names or in back of candidates' names. Granted, this argument is not compelled by the statutory language, but it seems the better reading.

There was, thus, a strong argument that the butterfly ballot violated Florida law. And the violation matched precisely with the evidence of voter confusion. That is, this was no free-floating violation, no mere technicality that did not appear to harm anyone. The stories told earlier, the affidavits filed, the "outcry" evidence from election day, the statistical surveys—all are precisely what one would expect from placing punch-holes both before and after candidates' names and from placing a minor party candidate's punch-hole over that of a major party candidate. If the ballot had placed all punch-holes on the right and had clearly listed the candidates in proper order, the confusion would not have existed. The legal question, though, was whether these violations of Florida law were enough to warrant a remedy.

The leading Florida case on contesting an election (and remember that voters as well as losing candidates can contest elections) is *Beckstrom v. Volusia County Canvassing Board*.[13] The facts of *Beckstrom* are not parallel to the Palm Beach facts, but the high court set forth a test that applies:

> [W]e are not holding that a court lacks authority to void an election if the court has found substantial unintentional failure to comply with statutory election procedures. To the contrary, if a court finds substantial noncompliance with statutory election procedures and also makes a factual determination that reasonable doubt exists as to whether a certified election expressed the will of the voters, then the court in an election contest . . . is to void the contested election even in the absence of fraud or intentional wrongdoing.[14]

Because the Bush victory was so narrow—he was certified the Florida winner with a 537-vote lead—the illegal butterfly ballot, which might have resulted in a few thousand votes going to Buchanan that were meant for Gore, certainly raised a "reasonable doubt . . . as to whether [the] certified election expressed the will of the voters." The harder question was whether the illegality of the ballot constituted "substantial noncompliance with statutory election procedures." "Substantial noncompliance" requires proving more than a mere legal technicality but doesn't require proving fraud. Where does the butterfly ballot illegality fall on this spectrum?

Judge Jorge LaBarga ruled against the plaintiffs, but he ruled neither on whether the butterfly ballot was illegal nor on whether any such illegality constituted "substantial noncompliance." Rather, he skipped straight to the remedy issue and concluded that, even if the ballot was in substantial noncompliance with Florida election law, he had no authority to order a new vote. Plaintiffs appealed Judge LaBarga's ruling directly to the Florida

Supreme Court,[15] and the high court unanimously affirmed, but on different grounds. With virtually no discussion, the court held that, "even accepting appellants' allegations, we conclude as a matter of law that the Palm Beach County ballot does not constitute substantial noncompliance with the statutory requirements mandating the voiding of the election."[16] So that was the end. Because of the cryptic nature of the court's ruling, it is impossible to know which aspects of the butterfly ballot it deemed problematic and which not. The defects, if any, did not constitute substantial noncompliance with Florida election law. After all, thousands of voters managed to negotiate the confusing ballot.

Perhaps, though, the high court took a peek at the remedial problems that would have arisen had it held the ballot in substantial noncompliance. An ideal remedy for the butterfly ballot situation would be to identify precisely which voters had mistakenly voted for Buchanan instead of Gore and award those votes to Gore, instead. The problem is that with a secret ballot—used everywhere in the country—it is impossible to trace which ballots fit the "meant for Gore, voted for Buchanan" description. A court could try to resolve this through voter affidavits, but that raises enormous problems regarding voter memory (can a voter who intended to vote for Gore clearly remember that he or she actually punched for Buchanan?) and voter fraud (false affidavits). Another possible remedy would be to rely on expert statisticians to determine how many of the 3,407 Buchanan votes were "really" Buchanan votes, but, as pleasing as that might seem as an academic project, there was zero chance any court would allow the presidential election to turn on such testimony. No, the only remedy would have been a new vote in Palm Beach County. But even if the revote were limited to just those voters who signed in on election day, and even if a revote would allow the erroneous Buchanan votes to become intended Gore votes, there was a major problem looming. Ralph Nader accumulated more than

5,000 votes in Palm Beach County, and it wouldn't take many Nader-to-Gore switches in a revote to hand the presidency to Gore. That seemed unfair to Bush. After all, Gore had the whole campaign to try to persuade the Nader voters to stick with the Democrat. Perhaps, though, a revote could have been arranged so that Bush and Nader (and all other minor party candidates other than Buchanan) would be locked in to their election night tallies, so that the revote would affect only the Gore and Buchanan numbers.

One can see the conundrum that would have faced the Florida Supreme Court had it ruled the butterfly ballot in substantial noncompliance with elections law. Perhaps that conundrum affected its ruling on the merits; it is impossible to know. However, after dismissing plaintiffs' claims on the merits, the high court said this about Judge LaBarga's ruling: "Because the dismissal [of plaintiffs' claims] would be proper on that basis [no substantial noncompliance], we conclude that all other issues ruled upon by the trial court were not properly reached and, therefore, the court's rulings thereon are a nullity."[17] In other words, Judge LaBarga's conclusions about his remedial powers were thrown out. Why did the high court do that?

Probably because one of Judge LaBarga's conclusions could have had dramatic consequences. He stated various reasons for holding that he lacked the power to order a revote, but one of those reasons was that, in his view, the Florida election contest provision—the provision that Gore was relying on to challenge Bush's certification as the winner and the provision the Palm Beach plaintiffs were using to seek a revote—did not apply to presidential elections. If that ruling stood, even though it was just the ruling of a trial court judge, it would have been powerful ammunition for the Bush team in fighting the Gore contest. But Judge LaBarga's reasoning was shaky, and it was not surprising that the Florida Supreme Court nullified his opinion.

Judge LaBarga's argument began with the uncontroversial proposition that the U.S. Constitution and federal law schedule the presidential election on a single day throughout the nation. The Constitution provides that "The Congress may determine the time for choosing the electors, and the day on which they shall give their vote; which day shall be the same throughout the United States."[18] Accordingly, Congress passed a law, which sets up presidential elections for the Tuesday following the first Monday in November, in each presidential election year.[19] What happens, though, if for some reason a law is violated in connection with a presidential election? Might another election take place, even if only in one state, even if only in one county, despite the constitutional and statutory language setting up a nationwide uniform presidential election day? Judge LaBarga answered No, but he did so in an indirect and ultimately unpersuasive fashion. He turned to another section of federal law—3 U.S.C. § 2. Section 2 provides that, if a state "has held an election for the purpose of choosing electors and has failed to make a choice on the day prescribed by law, the electors may be appointed on a subsequent day in such manner as the legislature of such State may direct." On its face, Section 2 constitutes a delegation from Congress to the states, permitting state legislatures to set forth a procedure for appointing electors on a day subsequent to the presidential election. Judge LaBarga maintained that the Florida legislature had not enacted any law setting forth such a procedure. More specifically, he concluded that the contest provision of Florida law, Section 168, was not such a procedure and "was not intended to apply to Presidential elections."[20] He concluded, "Congress clearly intended a procedure *other than* a second election in the event the electors were not elected on the date prescribed by law."[21]

Judge LaBarga may have been correct in that conclusion (although federal law is not clear on the subject), but two points he made along the way are highly questionable. First, his use of 3 U.S.C. § 2 overreads the importance of that provision. Congress almost certainly intended Section 2 for a narrow set of circumstances, in which a state literally does not make a choice on election day. Examples include the occurrence of a natural disaster that keeps voters from the polls, a breakdown of all the voting machines, or the failure of any candidate to receive a popular vote majority in a state that requires such a majority to get any electoral votes. The problem in the 2000 election in Florida was never that the state did not make a choice on election day. The problem was always the difficulty of figuring out which choice the Florida voters had made. Second, Judge LaBarga's conclusion that the Florida contest provision, Section 168, does not apply to presidential elections was based in part on the shaky premise that Section 168 is not the Florida legislature's method of carrying out its federally delegated Section 2 power. This is true, but beside the point, because Section 2 has nothing to do with revotes or with any other alleged legal problem that arises in a state after a presidential election. Section 2 covers situations in which a state has failed to make a choice on election day, not one in which it is trying to figure out the results of a choice it did make. Furthermore, Judge LaBarga's conclusion that the Florida contest section doesn't apply to presidential elections is based on still another shaky premise, that the section doesn't say anything about presidential elections. But neither does it exclude presidential elections from its otherwise broad scope.

It appears that the case went awry in part because of plaintiffs' choice of legal argument. The Palm Beach County plaintiffs had suggested to Judge LaBarga that the otherwise broad remedial power granted in the contest section of Florida law was the Florida legislature's way of carrying out its federal Section 2 power. The plaintiffs should have ignored Section 2, which doesn't apply here, and instead should have focused on the plain language of the Florida contest statute. That statute, Section 168, grants courts broad remedial power to correct legal wrongs. It has nothing to do with an arcane federal law that covers bizarre situations in which states actually fail to "make a choice" for president on election day.

11. Absentee Ballots

Seminole and Martin Counties and a Printer's Error

In October 2000, Sandra Goard, the elections supervisor for Seminole County, allowed Republican Party personnel to add voter registration numbers to incomplete requests for absentee ballots. That action, and a similar one by the Martin County elections supervisor, nearly cost George W. Bush the election. This chapter explores the Seminole and Martin County cases, against a backdrop of Florida's problems with absentee ballot voting.

As part of their get-out-the vote drives, both major parties sent preprinted absentee ballot request forms to their likely voters. The forms usually contain much of the information the applicant has to include by law, and then the applicant adds some other required information (such as his or her signature) and sends the form back to the county. If all the required information is on the form, the county will send the voter an absentee ballot. If any of the required information is missing, the county can try to contact the voter to correct the application, but it cannot issue the ballot.

For the 2000 election, the Democrats had no problems with their preprinted forms, but the Republicans did. Because of a printer's error, the forms sent to likely Republican voters included neither the voter's registration number nor a space to put that number, and the forms didn't tell the potential voters that a voter registration number was required. Thousands of forms came back to the Seminole County elections office missing voter registration numbers, and Supervisor Goard placed these forms along with others (containing different problems) in a rejected applications pile. When state GOP officials discovered the problem, they asked Goard for permission to take the rejected forms from their likely voters into a room at the supervisor's office and complete the applications by adding the correct voter registration numbers. Goard granted this request, and GOP representatives, not employed by the county, spent weeks at the county office adding the registration numbers, as a result of which thousands more absentee ballots were mailed to likely GOP voters. Goard didn't advise any other political parties of the GOP activity, nor did any other party request similar access to her offices and to rejected absentee ballot applications. The Democrats, of course, didn't need similar wholesale access, for there was nothing wrong with the Democrats' preprinted forms.

A virtually identical story occurred in Martin County, although there the GOP personnel were permitted to remove the rejected forms from the county offices entirely. After filling in the voter registration numbers on the forms, the GOP workers returned the forms to the supervisor's office, where the forms were then processed and the absentee ballots were mailed to the voters.

Some Democratic residents of Seminole and Martin Counties sued under Florida's election contest provision to invalidate all the absentee ballots cast as votes in those counties because of the GOP alteration of the otherwise rejected absentee ballot request forms. Such a remedy in Seminole County would have resulted in a net loss of around 5,000 votes for Bush; in Martin County, tossing all the ballots would have yielded a net loss of around

2,500 votes for Bush. In other words, if plaintiffs had won either case, Gore would have won the election. And Gore wasn't even party to the cases. He had made the strategic decision not to join these lawsuits where (a) plaintiffs were seeking to throw out votes, while in the punch-card county challenges Gore was asking to include votes and (b) some of the absentee ballots that would be tossed would be military votes, which Gore didn't want to be perceived as challenging.

The cases were tried separately, and the rulings were issued on Friday, December 8, just hours before the Florida Supreme Court allowed Gore's election contest to go forward. Judge Nikki Ann Clark, who rejected GOP requests to recuse herself because she had been passed over by Governor Jeb Bush for elevation to the appeals court, tried the Seminole case. Judge Terry Lewis—the same judge who ruled during the protest phase discussed in chapter 3 and who had jurisdiction over the contest phase, discussed in chapter 4, when the U.S. Supreme Court ended the election—tried the Martin case. To win either case, plaintiffs needed to show that the addition of the voter registration numbers violated Florida law. They then needed to show that the violation constituted "substantial noncompliance" with election law, as required by Florida caselaw. Finally, they needed to show that the appropriate remedy was the invalidation of all absentee ballots cast in the county or perhaps some less draconian remedy, such as the invalidation of a percentage of the ballots cast. In the end, plaintiffs in both counties prevailed on the first issue but not on the second, so they never got to the third. But the cases were close and were scary for the Republicans.

Florida law is clear on two things relevant to the Seminole and Martin cases. First, it states that "The supervisor may accept a written or telephonic request for an absentee ballot from the elector, or, if directly instructed by the elector, a member of the elector's immediate family, or the elector's legal guardian."[1] The law does not authorize requests from party officials. GOP personnel were not, that is, authorized to fill out absentee ballot request forms, either in whole or in part. Second, Florida law requires the person making a request for an absentee ballot to disclose nine pieces of information, including the "registration number on the elector's [i.e., voter's] registration identification card."[2] The thousands of forms that the counties had rejected but that were resuscitated by the GOP personnel lacked the required registration number. Put these two things together—requests may be made only by the voter or a member of the voter's family or the voter's legal guardian, and requests must include the voter's registration number—and it is easy to see that, by allowing the GOP to complete thousands of request forms, the elections supervisors had violated Florida law. Even Judges Clark and Lewis agreed with that.[3]

The next question was whether the violation constituted "substantial noncompliance" with Florida election law. To understand what Florida considers "substantial noncompliance"—and why a plaintiff needs to prove that, rather than merely any legal violation—one must look at four prior cases, in two of which elections were overturned because of problems with absentee ballot voting.

In a 1975 case, *Boardman v. Esteva*,[4] the Florida Supreme Court explained that it had sometimes required strict compliance with absentee ballot rules, and sometimes not. Upon reviewing the prior cases, the court said that strict compliance was not necessary. More generally, the court held that "a fundamental inquiry should be whether or not the irregularity complained of has prevented a full, fair and free expression of the public will."[5] The court said that, to determine whether irregularities should lead to voiding absentee votes, it would consider these factors:

(a) the presence or absence of fraud, gross negligence, or intentional wrongdoing;

(b) whether there has been substantial compliance with the essential requirements of the absentee voting law; and

(c) whether the irregularities complained of adversely affect the sanctity of the ballot and the integrity of the election.[6]

Boardman thus makes clear that merely technical violations of absentee ballot rules will not invalidate absentee votes. Something more serious must be shown, although the three factors leave much room for interpretation. What is "substantial compliance"? What "adversely affect[s] the sanctity of the ballot and the integrity of the election"? Applying the three-factor test to the facts in *Boardman,* the court refused to invalidate 429 absentee ballots whose outer envelopes were destroyed by county canvassing boards, thus preventing judicial review of certain technical requirements. The ballots themselves were in compliance with the law, so the court refused to throw them out.

One thing is clear. A 1998 Florida Supreme Court case, *Beckstrom v. Volusia County Canvassing Board,*[7] held that, to contest an election, a plaintiff does not have to show fraud or intentional wrongdoing. The second *Boardman* factor—substantial noncompliance with statutory voting procedures—may be enough to invalidate an election. So the combination of *Boardman* and *Beckstrom* yields this proposition: To throw out absentee ballots, a plaintiff must prove more than a mere technical violation of law but need not prove anything as serious as fraud. "Substantial noncompliance" is somewhere in between.

Boardman and *Beckstrom* didn't overturn elections, but two other cases did, and the Democratic plaintiffs in Seminole and Martin Counties were relying heavily on those cases. *Bolden v. Potter*[8] involved nothing more exalted than a county school board election, but the case reached Florida's high court, which upheld a trial court judgment overturning the results of the election. Bolden, who had lost, showed that some voters had been paid to cast absentee ballots, while other ballots had been "witnessed by the same persons who had witnessed the bought ballots and conducted the organized vote-buying operation."[9] This was real fraud and "affected the sanctity of the ballot and the public's perception of the integrity of the election."[10] The fraud "tainted the entire absentee-voting procedure,"[11] and all of the absentee ballots in the race were thrown out. Bolden was declared the winner.

The other case involved an election for mayor of the City of Miami.[12] Joe Carollo won the machine vote, but Xavier Suarez surged ahead on the absentee vote and took the oath of office as mayor. A few months later, however, a trial court found "massive absentee voter fraud which affected the electoral process."[13] The fraud included false voter addresses, stolen ballots, falsely witnessed ballots, and ballots procured or witnessed by ballot brokers. Although the trial court had ordered a new election as a remedy, the intermediate appellate court held instead that all the absentee ballots cast must be discarded. The vote accordingly reverted to the machine count, and the court declared Carollo the winner, ousting Suarez from the position.

The remedy in both *Bolden* and the *Miami Mayor Case*—throwing out all absentee ballots cast—traces back to language in the *Boardman* case, which itself cited even older Florida caselaw. Even though the *Boardman* court didn't throw out the 429 absentee ballots whose outer envelopes had been destroyed, it did say this:

> The general rule is that where the number of invalid absentee ballots is more than enough to change the result of the election, then the election shall be determined solely upon the basis of the machine vote. The reason for the rule is that since all the ballots have been commingled and it is impossible to distinguish the good ballots from the bad, because all ballots

are required by law to be unidentifiable, then in fairness all the ballots must be thrown out. In other words, it is impossible to tell for whom the invalid ballots were cast since they were commingled with the valid ballots.[14]

So, although the *Boardman* Court didn't throw out the 429 ballots in question, deeming the error involving the outer envelopes technical and not rising to the level of "substantial noncompliance," it did open the door to cases such as *Bolden* and the *Miami Mayor Case,* both of which threw out all absentee ballots because of the taint on some. These cases, in turn, opened the door to the claims in the Seminole and Martin County cases. If plaintiffs could convince the courts that the violations of Florida law amounted to "substantial noncompliance" with election law, then they would have a good argument to throw out all absentee ballots cast in those counties. The reason, as is clear from *Boardman,* is that it is impossible to tell which ballots ultimately cast resulted from the illegal absentee ballot applications, and thus the remedy, as approved for years by Florida courts, is to invalidate all absentee ballots in the county. They are all considered tainted by the illegality.

But plaintiffs never got that far, because neither trial judge found substantial noncompliance. That is, both judges found the facts to be closer to those of *Boardman*—technical violations that did not affect the integrity of the absentee ballots themselves—than to those of *Bolden* or the *Miami Mayor Case,* which involved proof of fraud, that is, vote buying, false witnessing, and the like. In addition, Judge Clark, in the Seminole County case, reasoned that Florida law renders "illegal" absentee ballots that do "not include the signature and the last four digits of the social security number of the elector" and either a notary's stamp or the attestation of a witness.[15] Although Florida law requires voters, their families, or guardians to place voter registration numbers on applications for absentee ballots, it does not render "illegal" improperly completed request forms as it does improper ballots themselves. Thus, Judge Clark held, "Unless a statutory provision also specifically states that the lack of information voids the ballot, the lack of the information does not automatically void the ballot."[16]

Judge Clark also turned away plaintiffs' argument that Supervisor Goard had treated the major parties unequally. Although only Republicans received access to incomplete absentee ballot request forms, the Democrats (a) didn't ask for such access and (b) didn't have a printer's problem with their preprinted forms. Goard's judgment was faulty, said the judge, but it "did not adversely affect the sanctity of the absentee ballots subsequently cast," and thus the certified election in Seminole County "was the result of the fair expression of the will of the people of Seminole County."[17] Judge Lewis's conclusions regarding the Martin County case were virtually identical. So the Democratic plaintiffs lost both cases at trial, and the only question was whether the Florida Supreme Court would view the issues differently.

It did not. In brief opinions issued Tuesday, December 12, hours before the U.S. Supreme Court dealt the final blow to Gore, the Florida Supreme Court unanimously affirmed the rulings of the trial judges.[18] In the Seminole County Case, it held: "We find competent, substantial evidence to support the trial court's conclusion that the evidence in this case does not support a finding of fraud, gross negligence, or intentional wrongdoing in connection with any absentee ballots."[19] It affirmed the Martin County ruling, on the basis of its holding in the Seminole County case.[20]

These two absentee ballot cases were serious ones, because the Democratic plaintiffs had clear evidence of violations of Florida law and of access to absentee ballot request forms granted to Republicans only. But the violations turned out to be more like a technical error than fraud. And the access, although unequal in a sense, was ultimately deemed not unequal because the Democrats didn't have a similar problem with their preprinted forms and hadn't asked the county supervisors for access to fix whatever forms from their likely voters might have been sitting on the discard pile. The remedy sought in each case—invalidation of all absentee ballots cast in the county—would have given the election to Gore, but the courts never reached the issue of remedy because they didn't deem the legal violation serious enough. One thought lingers from these cases, though. If plaintiffs had been able to identify precisely which ballots cast resulted from illegal supplementation of voter registration numbers, perhaps the courts would have thrown out those specific ballots. In other words, perhaps the looming draconian remedy—throwing out all ballots cast because of the taint on a few—affected the judges' rulings that the violations were not substantial. Perhaps the availability of a more precisely tailored remedy would have made it easier for the courts to deem the violations of law "substantial noncompliance." But the secret ballot that is a cornerstone of U.S. voting rights makes it impossible to trace which votes have been affected by election law violations. The inability to identify specific tainted votes makes remedies more difficult, because courts are reluctant to invalidate all ballots cast based on a violation regarding only some.

Part V. The Legislative Role

)

12. The Florida Legislature

What Was Its Proper Role?

When the U.S. Supreme Court ended the election on December 12, the Florida House of Representatives had already voted to appoint a slate of electors for George W. Bush, and the Florida Senate would have voted similarly the next day. The Senate never acted, because early on December 13, Al Gore told his Florida team to cease activities, that he would concede the election that night. From the beginning, the Florida legislature had loomed in the background of the election dispute. Early on, its GOP-controlled chambers made clear that they would not countenance a Gore victory in the state courts. If such a victory were to come, state legislative leaders broadly hinted that they would appoint a Bush slate in opposition. This chapter examines the arguments for and against the role the Florida legislature was about to play.

The federal Constitution delegates to state legislatures the power to determine the "manner" by which electors are chosen. All state legislatures currently have delegated to the people the power to choose electors. In no state today does law provide for legislative appointment of electors. No one disputes that the Florida legislature could, by law applicable to future elections, alter the state's "manner" of selecting electors. If it had the votes, the legislature could give itself the power to choose electors. Of course, the people of Florida might object to such a power grab and refuse to reelect some legislators, but if the legislature had the guts to take the election of a president away from the people, it could legally do so.

The problem in the 2000 election—at least for those advocating a separate, legislatively chosen slate of Bush electors—was that the Florida legislature had already provided by law for selection of electors via vote of the people. Here is the Florida statute:

> Electors of President and Vice President, known as presidential electors, shall be elected on the first Tuesday after the first Monday in November of each year the number of which is a multiple of 4. Votes cast for the actual candidates for President and Vice President shall be counted as votes cast for the presidential electors supporting such candidates. The Department of State shall certify as elected the presidential electors of the candidates for President and Vice President who receive the highest number of votes.[1]

So the Florida legislature could not rely on law already in existence to assume the power of appointing the electors itself. One could try to argue that the federal constitutional power to determine the "manner" of choosing electors is subject to revision at any time. That is, even if the people of Florida have voted on election day, the legislature could retroactively nullify that vote and pick its own electors. But no one seriously advanced this argument.

Instead, the Bush forces in the Florida legislature relied on yet another obscure provision of federal electoral college law. It is 3 U.S.C. § 2, and it reads: "Whenever any State has held an election for the purpose of choosing electors, and has failed to make a choice on the day prescribed by law, the electors may be appointed on a subsequent day in such a manner as the legislature of such State may direct."[2] That is pretty broad language, and the Florida legislature made the most of it. The legislature's basic position all along was that if Florida failed to resolve any judicial contest over the election by the safe-harbor date of December 12,[3] then Section 2 empowered the legislature to step in and appoint electors "in such a manner" as it may direct. In other words, the legislature construed the phrase "day prescribed by law" to refer not to election day, November 7, but rather to the safe-harbor date, December 12.

There are two major problems with that argument, however. The first is that the safe-harbor provision of federal law is not, by its own terms, an absolute rule. Rather, it is a conditional rule. If a state completes a judicial contest no later than December 12, then the state's electors are immune from challenge. But the safe-harbor provision does not require a state to complete a judicial contest by that date. December 18, the date on which federal law requires electors across the country to cast their votes for president, is a more likely candidate for the "day prescribed by law" for the state to "make a choice" of electors. On this reading, the Florida legislature's power of residual appointment of electors would not have kicked in unless December 18 arrived without Florida having finally chosen its electors.

The second major problem with the legislature's argument is that Section 2 was enacted in 1845, forty-two years prior to the Electoral Count Act of 1887 that established the safe-harbor provision.[4] Congress could not, therefore, have meant "day prescribed by law" to be the safe-harbor date. Section 2 was, however, enacted in conjunction with 3 U.S.C. § 1, which reads: "The electors of President and Vice President shall be appointed, in each State, on the Tuesday next after the first Monday in November, in every fourth year succeeding every election of a President and

Vice President."[5] It is likely that "day prescribed by law" in Section 2 refers to election day, the day established in Section 1, which was enacted along with Section 2. On this reading, a state legislature has the residual power of appointing electors if a state holds an election and fails to make a choice on election day.

How could that happen? As discussed earlier, a natural disaster could prevent the citizens from voting. Or voting machines could fail. Or perhaps state law might provide that electors go to the popular vote winner only if the winner gets a majority of the popular vote; if no candidate were to achieve such a majority, then the state would have "failed to make a choice." The point is that Section 2 was almost certainly envisioned as a fail-safe device against an array of possible election-day snafus. However, on November 7, 2000, Florida voters went to the polls; there was no natural disaster; machines generally worked (although they didn't always register votes well); Florida law is clear that the candidate who gets the most votes gets the state's electors. In other words, Florida's citizens made a choice on the day prescribed by law; the difficulty was figuring out what choice they made. Thus, there is a fairly strong argument that the Florida legislature had no appropriate role to play in appointing electors on its own.

One might respond, What if December 18 arrived, and the state still had not figured out who got the most votes? Even if Section 2 was written to refer to election day, surely it can be read to refer as well to some point down the road when the state risks losing its electors if the legislature doesn't act. Perhaps that is right, although it probably was not the intention of the 1845 Congress that wrote Section 2. Some would argue, though, that if Section 2 is indeed such a broad fail-safe provision, and does not refer simply to election day, then the legislature should wait until the last possible moment, which is not December 18, but rather early January, when Congress meets to count the electoral votes from around the country and declare a winner.

So there are essentially four possible positions:

1. The GOP argument, that if December 12 arrives and the judicial contest is not concluded, Section 2 gives the legislature the power to act

2. The narrowest position, that once a state has held an election on election day and is simply sorting out who won, the legislature has no role to play

3. An intermediate position, that the legislature must step in to ensure the state doesn't lose its electoral votes, and that the step-in date is December 18, when under federal law electors around the nation must vote for president

4. A second intermediate position, that the legislature must ensure against loss of electoral votes but must give a state's judicial process as much time as needed to finish, unless that process runs up against congressional counting of electoral votes early in January.[6]

There was never a need for determining which position was correct. Had the U.S. Supreme Court allowed the manual counting to continue, however, and had Gore finished ahead, then the Florida legislature would undoubtedly have offered up its own set of electors, for Bush. The next chapter explores how the U.S. Congress would have resolved such a conflict over electoral slates.

13. The U.S. Congress

The Unused Court of Last Resort

The framers of the Constitution envisioned an active role for Congress in choosing a president. Although they balked at making the president a direct appointee of Congress, they thought that a candidate would rarely receive an electoral vote majority and thus that the election would often be thrown to the House (to pick the president) and the Senate (to pick the vice president). The framers' vision proved shortsighted. Only two presidents have been chosen via the methods the framers set out (Jefferson, in 1800, and John Quincy Adams, in 1820), and only one other via a cobbled-together method (Hayes, in 1876). But the Constitution still provides a role for Congress in selecting a president, and federal law enacted in the wake of the Hayes-Tilden election envisions an expanded congressional role. This chapter discusses the legal ways that Congress could have been called upon to resolve the 2000 presidential election.

It is best to start with the federal law. As discussed earlier, the so-called safe-harbor provision, enacted as part of the Electoral Count Act of 1887, ensures that if a state concludes a judicial contest regarding a presidential election six days before the electoral college meets, the electors determined through the courts may not be later challenged. But that provision—3 U.S.C. § 5—was only one part of the Electoral Count Act, and by far the most straightforward part. There is also a much more complex section of that law, called, appropriately, "Counting electoral votes in Congress" and numbered 3 U.S.C. § 15. It could easily have become relevant in the 2000 election, for it covers different scenarios in which two slates of electors from the same state vie for recognition as the true or correct slate.

Section 15 begins with some ministerial issues and proceeds to the point where the President of the Senate (i.e., the Vice President of the United States)[1] announces the tally of the electoral votes from around the country. If at least one senator and one member of the House object in writing to the vote count and state their ground for objection, then the objection goes to both the Senate and the House, which sit separately. Section 15 then covers three different scenarios and sets out how each should be resolved. Each is described here, accompanied by an explanation of how it might have been brought into play in the 2000 election.

(1) The governor of the state in question might certify one electoral slate only and send that certificate to the National Archives, pursuant to 3 U.S.C. § 6. In that case, assuming the votes were "regularly" given by the state's electors, Section 15 instructs Congress not to reject the electoral votes. Only if both Houses of Congress, acting separately, agree that the votes were not "regularly" given can the electoral slate be rejected. The statute does not define "regularly" given, but it is generally understood that electoral votes simply need to meet constitutional requirements. The rule allowing Congress to reject votes not "regularly" given is not intended to give Congress carte blanche to reject an otherwise valid electoral slate because of policy or partisan differences with the candidate supported by that slate.[2]

In the 2000 election, after Secretary of State Harris certified Bush as the winner on November 26, Governor Jeb Bush sent to the National Archives the "certificate of ascertainment" indicating that his brother had won Florida's electoral votes. If there had been no contest to that certification, or if Bush had prevailed even after Gore's contest and any recounts, then this first scenario would have applied. With only one certificate of ascertainment, Bush would have won.

(2) What if, though, "more than one return or paper purporting to be a return from a state shall have been received by the President of the Senate"?[3] That is, what if two electoral slates present themselves to Congress? Section 15 covers this scenario. It says that, "those votes, and those only, shall be counted which shall have been regularly given by the electors who are shown by the determination mentioned in section 5 of this title to have been appointed."[4] Section 5 is the safe-harbor provision. That provision ensures that the electoral votes go to the slate determined through the state's judicial contest procedures, if the contest was completed at least six days prior to the meeting of the electoral college (i.e., no later than the "safe-harbor" date). The only exception to this rule is if two authorities in a state both purport to be the body that resolves contests over electors, and different candidates prevail in the two contests. The question then would be which body "is the lawful tribunal of the State."[5] Both Houses of Congress would meet separately, and if they agreed on which slate represents the state's lawful tribunal, then that would be the end of the matter. If they disagreed, then the slate certified by the state's governor, under his seal, would prevail.

This second scenario could have been brought into play in the 2000 election. If the U.S. Supreme Court had not issued its stay on Saturday, December 9, and if the manual recounts had concluded no later than December 12, with Gore ahead, then the Florida Supreme Court would have issued an order directing the secretary of state to certify the electors for Gore. The safe-harbor date would have been met. Section 15 instructs Congress to count "only . . . those votes" of an electoral slate determined through a judicial contest concluded by the safe-harbor date. Gore would have had a powerful argument that only his slate, ordered by the Florida Supreme Court, should count. His argument would have come not just from the Section 15 language but also from the safe-harbor language, which deems "conclusive" a judicial contest completed by the safe-harbor date. (And there would have been no serious argument that the Florida Supreme Court is not the "lawful tribunal" in Florida.)

This would have held regardless of what Secretary of State Harris or Governor Jeb Bush or the Florida legislature might have done. That is, assume Harris refused to follow a court order to certify the election for Gore (arguably an act of official disobedience). Or assume Jeb Bush refused to do his part (arguably another act of official disobedience) and send the resulting certificate of ascertainment (superseding the prior one favoring his brother) to the National Archives. Or assume the Florida legislature voted for a Bush slate of its own. If any one or more of these scenarios had occurred, so long as the judicial contest was concluded in Gore's favor no later than the December 12 safe-harbor date, Section 15 of the federal law (and the safe-harbor provision itself) clearly would have required Congress to count only the Gore electoral votes, and not any of the others. That is why Gore all along pushed for quick manual recounts and why Bush all along sought to stop or delay such recounts and in any event to drag out the proceedings. With Bush ahead after election night, and ahead after the November 26 certification, Gore could be assured of the victory only by pulling ahead for good in a manual recount completed no later than December 12.

(3) Suppose, though, that more than one slate of electors from a single state presents itself to Congress and that the safe-harbor date has come and gone without completion of a judicial

contest? Not surprisingly, Section 15 addresses just such a situation. Here is the relevant language:

> [I]n such case of more than one return or paper purporting to be a return from a State, if there shall have been no such determination of the question in the State aforesaid [i.e., the safe-harbor date passes without resolution of a judicial contest], then those votes, and those only, shall be counted which the two Houses shall concurrently decide were cast by lawful electors appointed in accordance with the laws of the State, unless the two Houses, acting separately, shall concurrently decide such votes not to be the lawful votes of the legally appointed electors of such State. But if the two Houses shall disagree in respect of the counting of such votes, then, and in that case, the votes of the electors whose appointment shall have been certified by the executive of the State, under the seal thereof, shall be counted.[6]

Throughout Section 15, Congress envisioned the two Houses of Congress acting separately but required agreement of the Houses for there to be legal effect. Congress did not intend to distinguish between the phrase "concurrently decide," which suggests that the Houses act jointly, and the phrase "acting separately, concurrently decide," which suggests that the Houses act separately. In both instances, the Houses act separately but need to agree to resolve any dispute.[7] Accordingly, if there are two competing slates of electors and the two Houses, acting separately, agree on which slate is the correct one, then the matter is resolved. But, if the two Houses cannot agree, then, according to Section 15's language, the state's Governor ("executive") breaks the tie.

Note that this method of resolving a presidential election is likely unconstitutional. There is a fairly strong argument that

Congress may not delegate the presidential selection power to state executives. Even if Congress may delegate power to state executives to implement federal legislation, giving a state's governor the power to determine a state's electors and, in a year such as 2000, the power to decide the presidency is an abdication of federal power and a dangerous concentration of power in the hands of a single official.

This delegation of power is likely unconstitutional for a separate reason. As discussed in chapters 6 and 7, the Constitution in Article II expressly delegates to state legislatures the power to determine the manner of choosing presidential electors. By giving this power to state executives, Section 15 arguably violates Article II.

The third electoral-slate scenario, like the second one, could have come to pass in the 2000 election. Assume that the U.S. Supreme Court, after holding the Florida manual counting system unconstitutional, had sent the case back to Florida, as Justices Souter and Breyer urged, to put in place a clear, uniform system for counting by hand. Assume further that the hand counting had continued past the safe-harbor date of December 12 but had concluded by December 18, when electors had to cast their votes for President.[8] If Bush had finished ahead, then there would have been no need to invoke Section 15, for he would have been the winner from the earlier certification and the winner after the statewide manual recount. But, if Gore had finished ahead and the Florida Supreme Court then had ordered Secretary of State Harris to certify Gore the winner, a number of different scenarios could have ensued, all but one of them resulting in Bush's winning Florida and, thus, the presidency.

Because the safe-harbor date would have passed, Gore would not have been able to invoke federal law to ward off challenges to a Democratic slate of electors. His only shot at victory would have come if Harris had followed the Court's order and certified

Gore as the winner, if Jeb Bush had followed, too, and sent that certification to Washington, and if the Florida legislature had backed off its pledge to appoint a slate of Bush electors. And perhaps this would have happened. After all, this scenario envisions the U.S. Supreme Court allowing the hand counting to continue under clear, consistent standards and envisions a Gore victory pursuant to such a U.S. Supreme Court ruling and under such standards. In that case, with the U.S. Supreme Court's stamp of legitimacy on the Florida process, there would have been enormous pressure on Bush to concede.

But, of course, he might not have conceded, and if, under this scenario, he had stayed in the race, he would have won on any hypothetical set of facts. Here are some:

(a) Assume Harris refused to certify the Gore slate. Then the prior slate—the Bush slate—would have competed in Congress, in January, with the slate ordered by the Florida Supreme Court—the Gore slate. With the safe-harbor date not having been met, the matter would have been thrown to both Houses of Congress. Assuming party-line voting, the new House, majority Republican like the prior House, would have chosen the Bush slate. The new Senate, split evenly between the parties, would have chosen the Gore slate, because the sitting Vice President (Gore) would have broken the tie.[9] With the two Houses disagreeing, Section 15 of the federal law breaks the tie by deferring to the slate certified under the seal of the state's executive. Jeb Bush would have been able to deliver the election to his older brother.

(b) The same story would have played out if Harris had agreed to certify the Gore slate, but Jeb Bush had refused to send that certification to Washington. Again, there would have been competing Gore and Bush slates; again, the tiebreaker would have gone to the slate certified by the governor; again, that would have been the earlier certified Bush slate.

(c)   In both of the first two scenarios, the Florida legislature would have been irrelevant, because, in both scenarios, its slate would have duplicated a Bush slate already in existence. There is, though, one scenario in which the Florida legislature would have made a difference. Assume that both Harris and Jeb Bush had followed the (hypothetical) order of the Florida Supreme Court awarding the state's electors to Gore. Assume, further, that the Florida legislature had appointed a slate of Bush electors and that Jeb Bush had signed such a bill.[10] In this scenario, both the Gore and the Bush slates would have had the seal of the governor of Florida, and thus the Section 15 tiebreaker would have been of no avail.

In that circumstance, the matter would have reverted back to the Constitution. The Twelfth Amendment, ratified in 1804, requires that, to be elected president, one must receive a "majority of the whole number of electors appointed."[11] One question is whether, if Florida's electoral slates were deadlocked, it would be appropriate to say that Florida had "appointed" electors. If a deadlock means no appointment of electors, then Gore would have won the presidency, for without Florida, he had a majority of the electors nationwide—267-246. But the better reading is that, under this scenario, Florida would have appointed two separate electoral slates (rather than zero slates). It's just that the federal law doesn't specify a second tiebreaker, once the governor's seal is affixed to both slates. So 270 would still have been the number of electoral votes needed to win the presidency, and, with neither candidate reaching that number, the Twelfth Amendment's own tiebreaker rules would have been brought to bear.

Lo and behold, those rules would have produced a Bush presidency and a Lieberman vice presidency. For the Twelfth Amendment breaks the presidential tie by authorizing the House of Representatives to pick the president, with each state's delegation of House members casting one vote. In the 107th Congress, which entered in January 2001, twenty-eight states were controlled by Republicans, so Bush would have prevailed. But the Twelfth Amendment has a different rule for picking a vice president. It authorizes the Senate to vote, not by state delegation but by individual member. With the Senate split 50-50 between the Democrats and the Republicans, the sitting vice president, Gore, would have broken the tie in favor of his running mate, Joe Lieberman. Thus: President Bush, Vice President Lieberman. And perhaps, in this closest of elections, that would have been the fairest outcome.

Finally, a few thoughts about Section 15, "Counting electoral votes in Congress." Because Section 15 is a law and not part of the Constitution, it can be amended or repealed, as any law can. In theory, Congress can scrap the procedures and replace them with others (so long as they don't violate the Constitution). Congress would, of course, need the president's signature to amend or repeal a law, or it would need to pass the new provision over the president's veto, which requires a two-thirds majority in both Houses.

There is a question whether Section 15 is constitutional. Congress does not have general power to act; it must point to a grant of power in the Constitution. Where did Congress get the power to pass Section 15? Surely not from the primary list of congressional powers in Article I, section 8 of the Constitution. Congress's power to determine results of electoral college voting comes initially from Article II, section 1, clause 3 of the Constitution and then from the Twelfth Amendment, which modified certain aspects of that clause. In both instances, although various procedures are set forth, the power to determine who won the election comes from this language: "votes shall then be counted." That sounds like a ministerial act: Count the votes. Section 15 goes far beyond the ministerial and authorizes Congress to resolve disputes among electoral slates through a variety of mechanisms. It is constitutional only if it is a reasonable interpretation of "votes shall then be counted." By granting discretionary, rather than ministerial, power to itself, Congress arguably violated the Constitution in enacting Section 15.

One response to this line of reasoning is that Section 15 was needed in the wake of the Hayes-Tilden election of 1876. That election ended after electoral slate disputes in three states could not be resolved under existing law. Congress had to put together an ad hoc commission to resolve the election. Thus, Section 15, coming along a decade later, fixed a hole in the electoral college scheme. If there was a hole, however, arguably it should have been fixed via constitutional amendment. That is the method the Constitution sets forth to deal with textual deficiencies.

Afterword

Was the 2000 presidential election resolved according to law, or was it all just politics? There is a rich tradition of legal scholarship suggesting that law is always just politics. The legal realists of the early to mid twentieth century, and the critical legal studies movement of the late twentieth century, each offered a critique of law's ability to move to a higher ground, to resolve conflict according to principle, rather than power. Principles, these critics argued, are endlessly manipulable, and which principles a judge uses to resolve a case are heavily, if not completely, influenced by that judge's political preferences.

This sort of critical approach to law dominated the discussion of the Supreme Court's landmark ruling, *Bush v. Gore*, which ended the 2000 election. Liberal critics charged that the conservative majority on the Court had manipulated conceptions of equal protection to invalidate the manual recounts in Florida. Further, the critics charged that the Court had manufactured a deadline of December 12 in the face of strong arguments that the counting could continue past that date. Politics, not principle, must have been behind these votes, or so maintained the critics from the left.

The liberals were not the only ones charging courts with playing politics. Conservative critics had been equally riled by the

Florida Supreme Court's rulings favoring Al Gore. When the state high court extended the manual recount period at the protest stage, and again when it awarded Gore a temporary reprieve at the contest stage, conservatives pointed to the Democratic affiliation of most of the Florida Supreme Court Justices and argued that those justices had stretched their interpretations of Florida law to favor the candidate they preferred.

In the wake of these critiques, I had to grapple with a core value in how I teach my classes. I seek to convey to my students that the law serves public ends, that it operates to improve the well-being of citizens, and that reasons, not politics, must govern in the interpretation of law. I have resisted the pull of legal realism and the critical legal studies movement—and similar views from the right that despair of the possibility of reason and principle in legal analysis. My approach is a combination of two beliefs: I believe the law to be constructed from and understood through reasoned analysis, and I want to believe and act as if that is the case, even when it is not. This latter approach is a variation on the many myths that society develops to cohere, rather than to fracture. We often act "as if" an overarching principle exists, to focus human energies that can otherwise easily turn to despair or to turmoil.

Although the sharp criticism of both the Florida and the U.S. high courts has made it harder to advance the view of law as a principled, relatively apolitical pursuit, the defense can still be made. It is often said that law is America's "civil religion." It is also, I believe, our way of avoiding the brutality of unmediated politics. Political struggle is just a step removed from real, literal struggle: human beings with vastly different notions of the good life thrown together in cities and towns, with violence always beckoning. Through politics, we allow representatives to do our bidding for us, and, if politics goes well, it can be accomplished peacefully. But, because political representation always looks back, just a step, to real struggles, it is always close to a kind of warfare. Law, on the other hand, is a genteel, some would say overly analytical, way of resolving disputes. The forms of law—pleadings, courts, judges, briefs, oral arguments—mask the true human struggles that lie underneath. But this is an important peacekeeping device. In 2000 we elected a president—the most powerful governmental official in the world—through a variety of legal mechanisms, in the face of intense partisan controversy. The election could easily have turned violent. That it did not is proof that law is the right form for resolving intense political disputes, regardless of what one thinks of the outcome.

If law becomes seen as nothing but politics, the moderating force of law is lost. Just as politics allows human conflict to be refracted through representation—we elect officials to govern and resolve disputes, rather than engaging in duels or blood feuds or other forms of vigilantism—so does law allow politics to be refined, removing us yet another level from the animating passions of human conflict. If the critics are right that the courts have eradicated the distinction between law and politics, we have lost another layer of protection against our less noble instincts.

The critics, though, are wrong. They have made a subtle, but understandable, mistake. What happened in Florida was this: Forms of law became exposed to an intense nationwide scrutiny. Anything upon which the entire nation's attention is turned, via the overwhelming resources of the contemporary media, will look scarred, imperfect, unclean. This is so whether the item under the microscope is a politician's sexual life, a famous athlete's alleged crime, or the system for electing presidents. The resolution of the 2000 presidential election turned on one state, and the resolution in that one state turned on an enormously complex interaction of politics and law. Of course, the law, under such scrutiny, will look imperfect and hard to distinguish from the politics. But that doesn't mean it is any less principled or that it serves any less as a peacekeeping device. When human beings (which is what judges are, after all) resolve tough questions with the nation and the world watching, it is impossible for the answers to look pure, uncorrupted, law-like. If the answers were easy—if there were a simple, straightforward rule of law that we all agreed applied and that we all agreed required resolution in favor of one candidate or the other—then the matter would have ended swiftly and would not have been all that interesting. Although there are many easy cases in the law (they often never reach court, resolved instead through settlement or plea bargain), the hard cases are the stuff of legal teaching and legal lore. *Bush v. Gore* and the other cases of the 2000 election were hard, and, under the camera's glare, it was hard to keep them from seeming political.

If the court critics are wrong for confusing the revealed blemishes of the legal system with the usurpation of law by politics, defenders of the legal system still have the burden of showing the judicial opinions to be principled. By principled I do not mean correct. One can vehemently disagree with a judge's reasoning and still accept the outcome as based in reason. Every important legal conclusion discussed in this book can be defended as at least based in reason. The Florida Supreme Court issued two controversial rulings favoring Al Gore, but both can be defended as reasonable readings of Florida law. Similarly, the rejection of the butterfly ballot case and the absentee ballot cases, which went against the Democrats, can also be understood through the application of principle, rather than politics. Finally, much of what the U.S. Supreme Court did in the 2000 election should be seen, even by Democrats, as based in plausible interpretations of the relevant legal materials. The first case, in which the Court unanimously remanded to the Florida high court for further explanation, followed many other Supreme Court cases in which the Court finds a method for ducking a difficult question. The second case, which ended the election, turned substantially on a concern with differential rules for counting votes county by county under a vague state standard. Whether that concern is best seen as one of equal protection or, as I have argued, as an offshoot of First Amendment cases focused on removing unconstrained discretion from government officials, the rejection of Florida's manual recount system was not a purely political act by the Court. It was based in reason.

The Supreme Court's decision to stop the election on December 12 poses the most difficult challenge for the thesis that all the rulings from the 2000 election were based in reason. As discussed in chapter 9, it is hard to defend the determination of the five-Justice majority that the Florida legislature had opted for December 12 as the last date for vote counting. Yet, even here, the majority opinion has the shape and sound of law. It refers to a federal statute that provides a safe harbor for states that complete election contests by December 12, and it takes heed of the state supreme court's reference to that safe-harbor provision. I have suggested that had the Court discussed all the Florida Supreme Court references to the safe-harbor provision, the best course would have been to remand to the state court for clarification, for there are indications that the state court erroneously deemed the safe-harbor provision to be mandatory, rather than conditional. But even though the Court's reasoning seems both inaccurate and incomplete, it nonetheless represents an attempt at construing the relevant legal materials. It amounts to an act of legal interpretation.

This one critical ruling exists at the outer edge of acceptable principled action, but we can still call it law. We can add to the final ruling the point that everything else about the five weeks of legal turmoil proceeded, even more clearly, in law-like fashion. Reasons were given that were defensible from statutory text or judicial precedent; opposing views were canvassed and rejected through argument; difficult questions were resolved by reference to principle, rather than politics. Instead of covering riots to resolve power struggles, the press was able to turn its cameras and microphones to courtrooms, judges, lawyers, and clerks of the court. The mediating force of law held, keeping violence at bay. We experienced, as a nation, another peaceful transition of government. It was a transition accomplished through the rough and tumble of politics, but also through the civilizing force of law.

Notes

NOTES TO THE INTRODUCTION

1. One Gore elector decided to cast no vote, as a protest, so the official certified electoral vote was 271-266.

NOTES TO CHAPTER 1

1. According to the census data from the end of 2000, California has 33,930,798 people, while Wyoming has 495,304 people. That is a ratio of about 68.54:1, or about 205:3. *See* www.electiondataservices.com.

2. U.S. Const., Art. II, § 1, cl. 4.

3. U.S. Const., Art. II, § 1, cl. 2.

4. U.S. Const., Amend. XII.

5. Because the new Congress is sworn in before the counting of electoral votes in Congress, any votes for president or vice president in the House or Senate under constitutional procedures would be done by the incoming Congress, rather than by the outgoing, or "lame duck," Congress.

6. II Records of the Federal Convention of 1787, at 501 (M. Farrand ed.) ("II Records").

7. *See* I Records of the Federal Convention of 1787, at 81 (M. Farrand ed.) ("I Records"); II Records, *supra* note 6, at 32; *id.* at 101, 121, 402.

8. Supporters of allowing Congress to pick the President included Sherman of Connecticut, *see* I Records, *supra* note 7, at 68; II Records, *supra* note 6, at 29; Rutledge of South Carolina, *see* I Records, at 69; II Records, at 57; Pinckney of South Carolina, *see id.* at 30; Houston of New Jersey, *see id.* at 99; Spaight of North Carolina, *see id.* at 99; Strong of Massachusetts, *see id.* at 100.

9. Supporters of an election by the people included Wilson of Pennsylvania, *see* I Records, *supra* note 7, at 68, 69, 80; II Records, *supra* note 6, at 30; Morris of Pennsylvania, *see id.* at 29–31; Madison of Virginia, *see id.* at 111; Carroll of Maryland, *see id.* at 402.

10. *See* Abner S. Greene, *Checks and Balances in an Era of Presidential Lawmaking*, 61 U. Chi. L. Rev. 123, 140–53 (1994).

11. Wilson of Pennsylvania appears to have been the first to propose it. *See* I Records, *supra* note 7, at 80. *See also id.* at 292 (electoral proposal by Hamilton of New York); II Records, *supra* note 6, at 404 (electoral proposal by Morris of Pennsylvania and Carroll of Maryland). Other proposals included: appointment, either of the president directly or of electors, by state executives (proposed by Gerry of Massachusetts, see I Records, at

175; II RECORDS, at 57); electors appointed by the state legislatures (proposed by Ellsworth of Connecticut and Broom of Delaware, *see id.* at 57; adopted at least temporarily by the Convention, *see id.* at 58).

12. For discussion of the origins of the electoral college, *see* JACK N. RAKOVE, ORIGINAL MEANINGS: POLITICS AND IDEAS IN THE MAKING OF THE CONSTITUTION 89–90, 259–60, 264–68 (1996).

13. *See* II RECORDS, *supra* note 6, at 497.

14. *See id.* at 525.

15. *See id.* at 527 (proposal of Williamson of North Carolina).

16. Alexander Hamilton, FEDERALIST PAPERS No. 68.

17. *See* William Josephson and Beverly J. Ross, *Repairing the Electoral College,* 22 J. LEGIS. 145, 184–85 (1996).

18. *See* JAMES MACGREGOR BURNS, THE WORKSHOP OF DEMOCRACY 67, 201–02 (1985).

19. U.S. Const., Art. V.

20. *See* Baker v. Carr, 369 U.S. 186 (1962), and Reynolds v. Sims, 377 U.S. 533 (1964).

NOTES TO CHAPTER 2

1. WEBSTER'S THIRD NEW INTERNATIONAL DICTIONARY 368 (1986).

2. Fla. Stat. § 102.166 (7)(b). The references in this book are to Florida election law as it existed in the fall of 2000.

3. Fla. Stat. § 101.5614 (5).

4. *See* for example Florida Democratic Party v. Palm Beach County Canvassing Bd. (11/22/00 opinion of Judge LaBarga).

5. *See* Cal. Elec. Code § 15627; Ind. Code § 3-12-3-13; Ken. Rev. Stat. § 117.383 (8); Mass. Laws § 135B; Minn. R. 8235.1000 (administrative regulation); § 115.585 (5) Rev. Stat. Mo.; Mont. Code § 13-16-414 (3); Rev. Stat. Neb. § 32-1119 (6); Nev. Rev. Stat. § 293.404 (3); N.J. Stat. § 19:53A-14; 26 Okla. Stat. § 8-111 (A); 25 Penn. Stat. § 3031.18; R.I. Gen. Laws § 17-19-37.1 (3); A.R. S. Dak. 5:02:09:05 (5) (administrative regulation); Rev. Code Wash. § 29.64.015 (1)(b); W. Va. Code § 3-4A-28 (4). Kansas, Maine, and Michigan also incorporate hand counting, but as part of the initial count. *See* Kan. Stat. § 25-4611 (e) and (f); 21-A Maine Rev. Stat. § 855-A (1); Mich. Stat. § 6.1798 (2).

6. Mont. Code. § 13-16-414 (3).

7. R.R.S. Neb. § 32-1119 (6).

8. Nev. Rev. Stat. § 293.404 (3).

9. R.I. Gen. Laws § 17-19-37.1 (3).

10. Rev. Code Wash. § 29.64.015 (1)(b).

11. W. Va. Code § 3-4A-28 (4).

12. Tex. Elec. Code § 127.130 (d) and (e).

13. Tex. Elec. Code § 212.005.

14. Darby v. State, 75 So. 411, 412 (Fla. 1917).

15. Delahunt v. Johnston, 671 N.E.2d 1241, 1243 (Mass. 1996).

16. McCavitt v. Registrars of Voters, 434 N.E.2d 620, 625 (Mass. 1982) (quotation, citations omitted).

17. Pullen v. Mulligan, 561 N.E.2d 585, 609 (Ill. 1990).

18. *Id.* at 609.

19. *Id.* at 611.

20. In re Election of the United States Representative for the Second Congressional Dist., 653 A.2d 79, 90 (Conn. 1994).

21. *Id.* at 90–91.

22. *Id.* at 92 (quoting Scully v. Westport, 145 A.2d 742 (Conn. 1958) (emphasis omitted)).

23. Hickel v. Thomas, 588 P.2d 273, 274 (Alaska 1978). *See also* Fischer v. Stout, 741 P.2d 217, 221 (Alaska 1987) (counting punch-card ballots marked by pen).

24. Wright v. Gettinger, 428 N.E.2d 1212, 1225 (Ind. 1981).

25. Moore v. Hayes, 744 P.2d 934, 941 (Okla. 1987).

26. Duffy v. Mortenson, 497 N.W.2d 437, 439 (S.D. 1993).

NOTES TO CHAPTER 3

1. Fla. Stat. § 102.141 (4).

2. Fla. Stat. § 102.166 (4)(a).

3. Fla. Stat. § 102.166 (4)(c).

4. Fla. Stat. § 102.141 (1).

5. Fla. Stat. § 102.141 (3).

6. Fla. Stat. §§ 102.111 (1) and 102.112 (1).

7. Fla. Stat. § 102.166 (4)(d).

8. Fla. Stat. § 102.166 (5).

9. Palm Beach County Canvassing Bd. v. Harris, 772 So.2d 1220, 1229 (Fla. 2000), *vacated and remanded by* Bush v. Palm Beach County Canvassing Bd., 121 S. Ct. 471 (2000), *on remand,* Palm Beach County Canvassing Bd. v. Harris, 772 So.2d 1273 (Fla. 2000).

10. There is a rule of construction that sometimes operates in these situations: "expressio unius est exclusio alterius," which means, The expression of one is the exclusion of the other. That is, by expressing a phrase in one spot and excluding it elsewhere, the legislature intends for that phrase not to apply where it doesn't appear.

11. McDermott v. Harris (slip op. 11/14/00 at 2–3).

12. McDermott v. Harris (slip op. 11/17/00 at 2).

13. Fla. Stat. § 101.67 (2).

14. Fla. Admin. Code § 1S-2.013 (7).

15. *Id.*

16. As required by Florida law, Gore filed his appeal in the intermediate-level appellate court, which immediately certified the appeal to the Florida Supreme Court as raising a question of great public importance. *See* Fla. Const. Art. V, § 3 (b)(5).

17. Fla. Stat. § 102.111 (1).

18. *Id.*

19. Fla. Stat. § 102.112 (1).

20. Palm Beach County Canvassing Bd. v. Harris, 772 So.2d 1220, 1234 (Fla. 2000) (*see* n.9, *supra,* for subsequent citation history).

21. Fla. Stat. § 102.112.

22. 772 So.2d at 1234.

23. Fla. Stat. § 101.5614 (8).

24. Fla. Stat. § 102.166 (7)(a).

25. Fla. Stat. § 102.166 (4)(b).

26. 772 So.2d at 1237, 1239.

27. More precisely, the electors meet to cast their votes on the first Monday after the second Wednesday in December. *See* 3 U.S.C. § 7. In 2000 that "electoral college" date was December 18. And if a state's electors are to be immune from challenge in Congress, any judicial contest involving the presidential election must be completed at least six days prior to the date the electors meet to cast their votes. *See* 3 U.S.C. § 5. In 2000 that "safe-harbor" date was December 12.

NOTES TO CHAPTER 4

1. 3 U.S.C. § 6.

2. Fla. Stat. § 102.168 (3).

3. Fla. Stat. § 102.168 (3)(c).

4. Gore v. Harris (transcript of 12/4).

5. As with the appeal in the protest phase, here, too, Gore filed the appeal in the intermediate-level appellate court, which immediately passed the case to the Florida Supreme Court, as permitted by Florida law in matters of great public importance. *See* Fla. Const. Art. V, § 3 (b)(5).

6. Gore v. Harris, 772 So.2d 1243, 1256–57 (Fla. 2000), *reversed and remanded by* Bush v. Gore, 121 S. Ct. 525 (2000), *on remand,* Gore v. Harris, 773 So.2d 524 (Fla. 2000).

7. The court acknowledged that perhaps the correct net gain was 176, from an audited total, and it asked the trial court on remand to resolve which number was correct. 772 So.2d 1243, 1248 n.6.

8. Fla. Stat. § 102.168 (8).

9. Fla. Stat. § 101.5614 (5).

10. *Id.*

11. Fla. Stat. § 102.166 (7)(b).

12. Fla. Stat. § 102.168 (8).

13. 772 So.2d 1243, 1262.

14. Beckstrom v. Volusia County Canvassing Bd., 707 So.2d 720, 725 (Fla. 1998).

15. 772 So.2d 1243, 1266.

16. *Id.* at 1266 n.28.

17. *Id.* at 1272.

18. Gore v. Harris (order 12/8/00).

NOTES TO CHAPTER 5

1. Fla. Stat. § 101.5614 (6).

2. Siegel v. LePore, 120 F. Supp. 2d 1041, 1050 (S.D. Fla.), *cert. denied,* 121 S. Ct. 510, *aff'd,* 234 F.3d 1163 (11th Cir. 2000) (en banc).

3. 120 F. Supp. 2d at 1051.

4. *Id.* at 1052.

5. *Id.*

6. *Id.*

7. *Id.* at 1054.

8. Touchston v. McDermott, 120 F. Supp. 2d 1055 (M.D. Fla.), *aff'd,* 234 F.3d 1133 (11th Cir. 2000) (en banc), *cert. denied,* 121 S. Ct. 749 (2001).

9. Touchston v. McDermott, 234 F.3d 1130 (11th Cir. 2000); *see also* Siegel v. LePore, 234 F.3d 1162 (11th Cir. 2000) (relying on the order issued in *Touchston*).

10. Siegel v. LePore, 234 F.3d 1163, 1177 (11th Cir. 2000).

11. Touchston v. McDermott, 234 F.3d 1133, 1143 (11th Cir. 2000).

12. Fla. Stat. § 102.166 (5).

13. Erie R.R. v. Tompkins, 304 U.S. 64 (1938).

14. Siegel v. LePore, 234 F.3d 1163, 1198 (11th Cir. 2000).

15. Touchston v. McDermott, 234 F.3d 1133, 1158 (11th Cir. 2000), and Siegel v. LePore, 234 F.3d 1163, 1191 (11th Cir. 2000).

16. Siegel v. LePore, 234 F.3d 1163, 1182 (11th Cir. 2000).

17. *Id.*

NOTES TO CHAPTER 6

1. 3 U.S.C. § 5.
2. 3 U.S.C. § 7.
3. U.S. Const., Art. I, § 1, cl. 2.
4. Erie R.R. v. Tompkins, 304 U.S. 64 (1938).

NOTES TO CHAPTER 7

1. U.S. Const., Art. VI, cl. 2.
2. 5 U.S. 137 (1803).
3. 146 U.S. 1 (1892).
4. *Id.* at 25 (emphasis added).
5. *See also id.* at 35.

NOTES TO CHAPTER 8

1. Bush v. Palm Beach County Canvassing Bd., 121 S. Ct. 510 (2000).
2. Brief for Respondent, Bush v. Palm Beach County Canvassing Bd., November 28, 2000, at 22.
3. Theodore Olson presented arguments for Bush; Laurence Tribe did so for Gore.
4. Bush v. Palm Beach County Canvassing Bd., 121 S. Ct. 471, 473 (2000).
5. *Id.* at 474.
6. *Id.* at 475.
7. *Id.* at 474.
8. *Id.* at 475.
9. *Id.* (quoting Minnesota v. National Tea Co., 309 U.S. 551, 555 (1940)).
10. 121 S. Ct. at 475.
11. Palm Beach County Canvassing Bd. v. Harris, 772 So.2d 1273, 1289 (Fla. 2000).
12. *Id.* at 1290.
13. *Id.* at 1289.

NOTES TO CHAPTER 9

1. Bush v. Gore, 121 S. Ct. 512, 512 (2000).
2. *Id.* at 513.
3. *Id.* at 512.
4. *Id.*
5. Brief for Petitioners, Bush v. Gore, December 10, 2000, at 48.

6. *Id.*

7. Theodore Olson once again argued for Bush; this time David Boies presented arguments for Gore.

8. Bush v. Gore, 121 S. Ct. 525, 529 (2000).

9. *Id.*

10. *Id.* at 530.

11. *Id.*

12. *Id.*

13. *Id.* at 531.

14. *Id.* at 532.

15. *Id.*

16. *Id.* at 532–33.

17. *Id.* at 533.

18. If the U.S. Supreme Court had sent the case back to the Florida Supreme Court for implementation of constitutional vote-counting standards, would such standards be considered new law, not in existence as of the date of the election, and thereby raise once again Bush's initial set of arguments, as discussed in chapters 6 and 8? Probably not, for two reasons. First, courts frequently engage in interpretation of vague statutory provisions, and such interpretation is almost never considered "new law." It is considered statutory construction and is a common aspect of judicial practice. Second, it would be hard to argue that the Florida Supreme Court would be violating the law by implementing constitutional vote-counting standards if ordered to do so by the U.S. Supreme Court!

19. *Id.*

20. Chief Justice Rehnquist thought otherwise, writing, "Surely when the Florida Legislature empowered the courts of the State to grant 'appropriate' relief, it must have meant relief that would have become final by the cut-off date of 3 U.S.C. § 5." 121 S. Ct. at 538. Rehnquist cited no legislative history to support this claim, and the state law to which he referred, Fla. Stat. § 102.168 (8), makes no reference to the safe-harbor provision of federal law.

21. 772 So.2d 1273, 1286 n.17.

22. *Id.* at 1290 n.22.

23. 772 So.2d 1243, 1261 n.21.

24. *Id.* at 1262 n.22.

25. 121 S. Ct. at 534.

26. *Id.* at 538.

27. *Id.* at 540.

28. *Id.* at 541.

29. *Id.* at 542.

30. *Id.* at 543.

31. *Id.* at 545.

32. *Id.* at 550.

33. *Id.* at 556.

34. *Id.* at 557.

35. *Id.* at 531 (citing Gray v. Sanders, 372 U.S. 368 (1963)).

36. 121 S. Ct. at 531 (2000) (citing Moore v. Ogilvie, 394 U.S. 814 (1969)).

37. *See* Lovell v. Griffin, 303 U.S. 444 (1938); Schneider v. State, 308 U.S. 147 (1939); Largent v. Texas, 318 U.S. 418 (1943); Saia v. New York, 334 U.S. 558 (1948); Niemotko v. Maryland, 340 U.S. 268 (1951); Kunz v. New York, 340 U.S. 290 (1951); Staub v. City of Baxley, 355 U.S. 313 (1958); Shuttlesworth v. City of Birmingham, 394 U.S. 147 (1969); City of Lakewood v. Plain Dealer Publishing Co., 486 U.S. 750 (1988).

38. Gore v. Harris, 773 So.2d 524, 526 (Fla. 2000).

39. *Id.* at 527.

40. *Id.* at 529 n.12.

41. *Id.* at 537.

NOTES TO CHAPTER 10

1. *CNN Live Event/Special,* David S. Lee, University of California/Berkeley (transcript of 11/10/00).

2. Fla. Stat. § 101.5614 (6).

3. Material for the background story on Palm Beach and the statistical analyses drawn from: Daniel DeVise, Geoff Dougherty, and Andres Viglucci, *Palm Beach Voting Confusion Ends in "Statistical Anomaly,"* MIAMI HERALD, November 9, 2000; Rick Bragg and Dana Canedy, *The 2000 Election: Confused by the Ballot: Anger and Chagrin After an Oops on a Ballot,* NEW YORK TIMES, November 9, 2000, page A1; Bob Markey II, *Palm Beach County "Ground Zero": Democrats Said That Because of the Ballot Design, Thousands of Voters Mistakenly Voted for Pat Buchanan,* STUART NEWS/PORT ST. LUCIE NEWS, November 9, 2000, page A1; *CNN Live Event/Special,* November 10, 2000; Don Van Natta, Jr., and Dana Canedy, *Lawsuit Calls for Palm Beach Runoff Vote,* INTERNATIONAL HERALD TRIBUNE, November 10, 2000, page 1; Dexter Filkins, *Counting the Vote: Palm Beach County: Local Officials Say System Failed on Election Day,* NEW YORK TIMES, November 11, 2000, page A11; Don Van Natta, Jr., and Michael Moss, *Counting the Vote: The Nerve Center: Democratic "War Room" Tries to Oversee the Battle for Florida, to Mixed Results,* NEW YORK TIMES, November 11, 2000, page A12; Sue Ann Pressley and George Lardner, Jr., *In a Confused Palm Beach County, Complaints Came Early and Often,* WASHINGTON POST, November 11, 2000, page A01; Carol Marbin

Miller and Jason Grotto, *Elderly Jewish Voters Say They Were Confused by Butter-fly Ballot*, MIAMI HERALD, November 14, 2000; Don Van Natta, Jr., *Counting the Vote: The Ballot: Gore Lawyers Focus on Ballot in Palm Beach County*, NEW YORK TIMES, November 16, 2000, page A29; Frank Cerabino, *Large Vote for Buchanan Didn't Add Up: The Votes Coming from Heavily Jewish and Black Areas Didn't Make Sense*, PALM BEACH POST, December 17, 2000, page 8K.

4. Fla. Stat. § 101.5603 (4).

5. Fla. Stat. § 101.151 (3)(a).

6. Fla. Stat. § 101.151 (4).

7. Fla. Stat. § 101.151 (5).

8. The rules are repeated in display format in a separate section of Florida election law that is not by terms limited to paper ballot counties. *See* Fla. Stat. § 101.191. But the display, under the heading "Form of general election ballot," tracks the paper ballot requirements verbatim, so the legislature evidently intended it to be an example of how paper ballots should look. Ballots in counties with machines are expected to conform when possible to paper ballots, so section 101.191 can be used as a guide to ballots across the board.

9. Fla. Stat. § 101.151.

10. Fla. Stat. § 101.5609 (1).

11. Fla. Stat. § 101.5609 (2).

12. Fla. Stat. § 101.5609 (6).

13. 707 So.2d 720 (Fla. 1998).

14. *Id.* at 725.

15. As in most other cases during this postelection drama, the intermediate appellate court passed the appeal through to the Florida Supreme Court, which may exercise direct appellate jurisdiction in matters of great public importance. *See* Fla. Const. Art. V, § 3(b)(5).

16. Fladell v. Palm Beach County Canvassing Bd. (slip op. 12/1/00 at 3–4).

17. *Id.* at 4.

18. U.S. Const., Art. 2, § 1.

19. 3 U.S.C. § 1.

20. Fladell v. Florida Elections Canvassing Comm'n (slip op. 11/20/00 at 15).

21. *Id.* at 16.

NOTES TO CHAPTER 11

1. Fla. Stat. § 101.62 (1)(b).

2. Fla. Stat. § 101.62 (1)(b)(4).

3. Jacobs v. Seminole County Canvassing Bd. (slip op. 12/8/00 at 7); Taylor v. Martin County Canvassing Bd. (slip op. 12/8/00 at 4).

4. 323 So.2d 259 (Fla. 1975).

5. *Id.* at 265 (emphasis omitted).

6. *Id.* at 269.

7. 707 So.2d 720 (Fla. 1998).

8. 452 So.2d 564 (Fla. 1984).

9. *Id.* at 565.

10. *Id.* at 567.

11. *Id.* at 565.

12. In re: Protest of Election Returns and Absentee Ballots in the November 4, 1997 Election, 707 So.2d 1170 (Fla. Dist. Ct. App. 3d Dist.1998) ("Miami Mayor Case").

13. *Id.* at 1172.

14. 323 So.2d at 268.

15. Fla. Stat. § 101.68 (2)(c)(1).

16. Jacobs v. Seminole County Canvassing Bd. (slip op. 12/8/00 at 6).

17. *Id.* at 10.

18. Once again the appeals were passed through the intermediate appellate court directly to the state supreme court as constituting matters of great public importance. *See* Fla. Const. Art. V, § 3 (b)(5).

19. Jacobs v. Seminole County Canvassing Bd., 773 So.2d 519, 523 (Fla. 2000). The language of the court's ruling raises a complex question. The court did not apply the "substantial noncompliance" test from *Boardman* and *Beckstrom.* It is possible that the 1999 statutory amendments to the contest provision of Florida election law supersede these cases and that the court was relying solely on those amendments. The court was not clear on this subject. Note that in the final ruling in the Palm Beach County butterfly ballot case, *see* text accompanying note 16 (chapter 10), the Florida Supreme Court did apply the "substantial noncompliance" test.

20. Taylor v. Martin County Canvassing Bd., 773 So.2d 517 (Fla. 2000).

NOTES TO CHAPTER 12

1. Fla. Stat. § 103.011.

2. 3 U.S.C. § 2.

3. Legislative leaders referred to the judicial contest being completed *by* December 12, that is, by midnight the night before, but in fact the federal safe-harbor provision refers to judicial contests being completed "at least six days prior to" December 18. 3 U.S.C. § 5. So the safe harbor would be

reached so long as the judicial proceedings wrapped up no later than December 12, not midnight the night before.

4. An "amicus curiae" (i.e., "friend of the court") brief submitted by the Florida legislature to the U.S. Supreme Court incorrectly stated that Section 2 was passed as part of the Electoral Count Act of 1887. Brief of the Florida Senate and House of Representatives as *Amici Curiae* in Support of Neither Party, Bush v. Palm Beach County Canvassing Bd., November 27, 2000, at 5.

5. 3 U.S.C. § 1.

6. As precedent for this, note that in the 1960 election Hawaii submitted a revised electoral slate early in January, and it was accepted by Congress. *See* Josephson and Ross, *supra* note 17 (chapter 2), at 166 and n.154 (1996).

NOTES TO CHAPTER 13

1. U.S. Const., Art. I, § 3, cl. 4.

2. *See* Beverly J. Ross and William Josephson, *The Electoral College and the Popular Vote,* 12 J.L. & POLITICS 665, 729, 739 (1996).

3. 3 U.S.C. § 15.

4. *Id.*

5. *Id.*

6. *Id.*

7. For support of this reading, *see* Josephson and Ross, *supra* note 17 (chapter 2), at 182 and n.277.

8. It is possible that the counting could have continued past December 18 and still have been considered valid. Although federal law, 3 U.S.C. § 7, says the electors must meet on the first Monday after the second Wednesday in December—in 2000, December 18—the law is silent as to what happens if a state is not finished counting votes by that date. Perhaps the counting could continue until Congress meets early in January to count electoral votes from around the country. There is precedent for this from the 1960 election, when Hawaii changed its electoral slate after a recount and submitted the new slate to Congress, which accepted it early in January. *See* Josephson and Ross, *supra* note 17 (chapter 2), at 166 and n.154. But this did not affect the results of the election, and the President of the Senate, Vice President Nixon, who had lost the race to Senator Kennedy, accepted the new tally while making clear it should not necessarily serve as precedent.

9. The new Congress was sworn in on January 3, 2001, with Clinton and Gore still in office as president and vice president, until January 20, 2001. Electoral votes were counted during that seventeen-day window, and, had

the election been thrown into the Congress, Gore would have broken any Senate ties.

10. Had Governor Jeb Bush let the bill become law without his signature, by waiting seven days as is permitted under the Florida Constitution, *see* Fla. Const. Art. III, § 8(a), that would have created a Gore victory, because only the Gore slate, under this scenario, would have been certified by the governor.

11. U.S. Const., Amend. XII.

Acknowledgments

Many people played a role in making this book happen. During the critical five-week period late in 2000, when the focus was on Florida, I benefited from a series of discussions about the legal issues with my Fordham colleagues Martin Flaherty and Terry Smith and with my long-time friend and debating companion, John Nagle, of Notre Dame Law School; from terrific questions from my students in Criminal Law and in Freedom of Speech and of the Press; from the tremendous efforts of Lisa Finnegan and others at the Fordham Public Affairs office; and from a wonderful group of journalists at ABC News Radio (Tony Gatto, Steve Cohen, Peter Seligman, Jeff Fitzgerald, Ryan Kessler, and Bettina Gregory), who welcomed me as part of their team.

In getting this book from conception to publication, I was helped by Elizabeth Sheinkman, Seth Dubin, Milly Marmur, Thane Rosenbaum, Dan Elish, Kay Murray, Andrew Solomon, Don Rubin, Jeff Bolton, Bill Dworkin, Ted Slate, Jack Balkin, Steve Shiffrin, Richard Epstein, Cass Sunstein, Jesse Choper, Neal Devins, Jean Smith and Dan Auld from the faculty secretaries office, and Kate McLeod from the law school library. Great thanks as well to my editor, Jennifer Hammer, for her careful eye and thoughtful suggestions. I am grateful to Ellen Dubin for the jacket photo. I greatly appreciate the help of my colleague Bill Treanor, for his comments based on a close reading of the entire manuscript. Other colleagues who contributed in various ways, from reading manuscript drafts to discussing the election to providing moral support, include Ted Neustadt, Matt Diller, Ben Zipursky, Peter Siegelman, Jim Fleming, Tracy Higgins, Chantal Thomas, Jim Kainen, and our dean, John Feerick. I also want to thank Matt Shapiro, Dave Daskal, Derrick Widmark, and Carole Chervin for their supportive friendship throughout this process.

Finally, love and thanks to my mother, Judy Greene, and to my sister, Becky Greene. Together, the three of us keep alive the memory of my father, Phil Greene, a wonderful, loving man to whom this book is dedicated. My only regret is that he isn't around to read it.

Index

Absentee ballots: military, 48–49; Seminole and Martin County lawsuits, 9–10, 151–59
Adams, John Quincy, 21, 22, 168
Anderson, R. Lanier, III, 81
Antoon, John, II, 76

Baker, James, 42
Beckstrom v. Volusia County Canvassing Board, 144–45, 155, 194n. 19
Birch, Stanley, Jr., 78, 80–81
Boardman v. Esteva, 154–57, 194n. 19
Boies, David, 191n. 7
Bolden v. Potter, 155–57
Breyer, Stephen, 8, 111, 112, 117, 127–31, 173
Broward County: counting of chads, 56; manual recount, 43, 47, 55, 56, 58; overvotes, 140
Buchanan, Pat, 139–41, 143–45, 146–47
Burr, Aaron, 21
Bush, George W., *passim;* as president-elect, 131; election night, 2–3; son of President, 21; wins presidency, 121
Bush, Jeb, 3, 50, 58, 134, 153, 169, 171, 174–75
Bush v. Gore, 3, 8–9, 111–34, 178–83
Butterfly ballot, 2, 9, 137–50; image of, 138
Butterworth, Bob, 46–47, 49, 79

Carnes, Edward, 78, 80–81
Chads, 4; definition of, 30; dimpled (indented), 32–33, 36, 37–38, 39, 56–57, 71–72, 129; hanging, 31, 32, 36, 41, 71, 129; swinging, 32, 36, 171; tri-chad, 32–33, 71
Cheney, Dick, 78
Clark, Nikki Ann, 153, 154, 157–58
Cleveland, Grover, 22
Congress (United States) and resolution of electoral disputes, 10, 168–77, 185n. 5
Constitution (United States): Article V, 23, 25; Article II, 7, 16, 79, 85–93, 94–99, 101–7, 115, 126–27, 128–29, 130,

163–64, 172–73, 191n. 18; due process, 72, 74, 115–16; electoral vote, 3–4, 15–18; equal protection (manual recount in selected counties), 67, 72–73, 74, 78, 80–82; equal protection (voter's intent standard), 72, 74, 81–82, 86, 111, 115–16, 116–20, 127, 129, 129–30, 130, 131–33, 182; Fifteenth Amendment, 23; First Amendment, 77, 132–33, 182; presidential election day, 148; Seventeenth Amendment, 23; Twelfth Amendment, 17, 21, 130, 175–77; Twenty-Fourth Amendment, 23; Twenty-Sixth Amendment, 23; Twenty-Third Amendment, 17
Contest. *See* Election contest
Crawford, Bob, 50

December 18, and casting of electoral votes, 8, 54, 87, 120, 129, 130, 165–67, 173, 188n. 27, 195n. 8
December 12, and safe-harbor date. *See* Safe-harbor provision of federal law
District of Columbia, 17–18
Double-punched ballots. *See* Overvotes
Dubina, Joel, 78, 80–81

Election contest, 5–6, 49, 54, 56–69, 75, 80, 92, 99, 100, 106–7, 111–12, 124; trial, 63–64
Election protest, 4–5, 43–55, 91
Elections canvassing commission, 50
Electoral Count Act of 1887, 87, 165, 168–69, 195n. 4
Electoral vote, 2, 3–4, 15–26; arguments for its abolition, 22–26; constitutional rules, 15–18; counting in Congress, 112–13, 130, 131, 168–77; framing of the Constitution, 18–20, 168; unusual presidential elections, 20–22
Eleventh Circuit (federal court of appeals), 5, 76–82

Faithless electors, 16, 26, 185n. 1
Federal courts and state elections, 74, 79, 89–90, 104, 112, 115, 127, 130

About the Author

Abner Greene is a professor at the Fordham University School of Law. He specializes in constitutional law and has written extensively about the First Amendment and the separation of powers. During the five weeks between election night 2000 and the ultimate resolution of the election in favor of George W. Bush, Greene made more than eighty appearances in a wide array of television, radio, and newspaper venues. He became the ABC News Radio regular legal analyst, appeared on *ABC World News Tonight,* CNN, NPR *Talk of the Nation,* and C-SPAN, and was quoted on several occasions in the *New York Times.* Greene clerked for Supreme Court Justice John Paul Stevens in the 1987 and 1988 Terms and clerked for then Chief Judge Patricia M. Wald, of the United States Court of Appeals for the District of Columbia, during the 1986 Term.